EDITORIAL RESEARCH REPORTS ON

JOBS

FOR AMERICANS

Timely Reports to Keep
Journalists, Scholars and the Public
Abreast of Developing Issues, Events and Trends

Published by Congressional Quarterly, Inc.
1414 22nd Street, N.W.
Washington, D.C. 20037

D1279764

About the Cover

The cover was designed by Art Director Richard Pottern, who also provided many of the graphics in this book.

Editor, Hoyt Gimlin
Editorial Assistants, Barbara Cornell, Diane Huffman
Production Manager, I. D. Fuller
Assistant Production Manager, Maceo Mayo

Library of Congress Cataloging in Publication Data

Congressional Quarterly, inc.
   Editorial research reports on jobs for Americans.

   Bibliography: p.
   Includes index.

   1. Labor supply—United States—Addresses, essays, lectures. 2. Manpower policy—United States—Addresses, essays, lectures. 3. Labor and laboring classes—United States—Addresses, essays, lectures.
I. Title. II. Title: Jobs for Americans.
HD 5724.C725 1978   331.1'1'0973   77-18994
ISBN 0-87187-120-3

Contents

Foreword

The protection of American jobs from foreign competition is an old theme in U.S. history. But it has not been a dominant theme since World War II, when western industrial nations embarked on an unprecedented quarter-century of prosperity. This prosperity owes a large debt to a relatively unencumbered movement of trade on a massive scale between nations. But recent years have not been nearly so kind. The Arab oil embargo of 1973-74 and resulting oil-price increases touched off a global recession from which many European countries have been slow to recover.

Unemployment has approached politically unacceptable levels on both sides of the Atlantic—and with it has arisen a strong urge to protect home industries from foreign competition. In the United States, steel and textiles are among the most visible industries crying out for protection. Jobs are at stake, and organized labor is sympathetic to these cries. In Congress and in international trade negotiations, these pressures are being felt.

Aside from the protection of jobs from foreign workers—through imports or immigration restrictions—there is competition among various segments of the American public for the jobs that are available. Women are entering the work force at the highest rate in history. Older citizens have won congressional approval of their demand that they be allowed to work beyond age 65 if they so choose. And there are the chronic problems of youth unemployment, jobs for minorities, and welfare for those who cannot work.

Nine reports issued by Editorial Research Reports since the spring of 1976 survey the manifold facets of these problems and, we hope, throw some light on how the nation's policymakers are responding to them.

Hoyt Gimlin
Editor

January 1978
Washington, D.C.

JOB PROTECTION AND FREE TRADE

by

Jane A. Meyer

**Dec. 16
1 9 7 7**

JOB PROTECTION AND FREE TRADE

A MERICANS ARE BUYING imported goods in greater quantities and dollar amounts than ever before. At the same time, jobs in many domestic industries are in jeopardy—or have been lost—as a result of foreign competition. The convergence of these trends has created an important policy issue—how much government protection can and should be given to American industries threatened by foreign imports? There are no simple answers. Freer and expanded international trade would benefit many segments of the U.S. economy. At the same time, already high unemployment rates and fear of future increases have resulted in mounting pressure on the Carter administration and Congress to restrict imports.

AFL-CIO President George Meany recently declared: "Free trade is a joke and a myth. And a government trade policy predicated on old ideas of free trade is worse than a joke—it is a prescription for disaster. The answer is fair trade, do unto others as they do to us—barrier for barrier—closed door for closed door."[1] The 900 delegates to the AFL-CIO's biennial convention, held earlier this month in Los Angeles, approved—without dissent—a resolution calling for import quotas, curbs on business investment abroad and other stringent protectionist measures.

Those whose jobs and businesses are threatened by imports claim that American industries are at an unfair disadvantage because foreign manufacturers (1) pay lower wages and taxes, (2) do not have to comply with health, safety and environmental standards as stringent as American ones, and (3) can raise capital more cheaply and easily because of government assistance. Those whose standards of living and livelihoods depend on the availability of imports see the other side as chauvinistic and shortsighted. The lines cross and blur.

The American assembler of foreign-made electronic equipment may buy more American-made products than the average citizen. The American textile worker whose job is in jeopardy may own a Japanese television set—perhaps one not identifiably foreign-made, but one sold under an American name by an American department store or discount house. The steel

---

[1] Remarks made Dec. 8, 1977, in Los Angeles at the opening session of the national convention of the AFL-CIO.

worker who has just been laid off may be wearing a pair of Korean or Brazilian-made shoes, bought because they are cheaper than shoes made in the United States.

Mounting Pressure to Restrict Imports

The list of U.S. industries that have suffered from foreign competition in the last few years includes shoes, textiles, automobiles and television sets. Now steel has been added to the list. Employment in the steel industry has fallen from about 500,000 in the mid-1960s to about 365,000 workers today. Since last July some 20,000 steel workers have lost their jobs due to layoffs and plant shutdowns. So far this year more than 50,000 steelworkers have been certified by the Department of Labor as eligible for assistance under the Trade Expansion Act of 1974 *(see p. 6)*. This means that they receive periodic cash payments while looking for new jobs.

Steel plant closings in Youngstown, Ohio, Lackawanna, N.Y., and Johnstown, Pa., caused a loss of 12,000 jobs. In cities like these, where the steel industry is a major employer, the impact of plant closings is felt by many other businesses. In the Johnstown area the unemployment rate jumped from about 6 per cent to nearly 17 per cent after the Bethlehem Steel Corp. shut down its mill there last August. The immediate cause of the mill's closing was the disastrous flood Johnstown suffered a few weeks earlier. But it was the inability of that plant to compete with imported products that made the company decide not to repair and reopen it.

In recent months, businesses and labor groups that feel threatened by imports have become increasingly vocal about their problems. Zenith Radio Corp. workers in Chicago staged a downtown march in mid-October protesting the company's decision to lay off 5,600 workers and move substantial parts of its operation abroad. A few weeks later, steelworkers presented President Carter with petitions asking for continued import quotas on specialty steel. The petitions bore over 100,000 signatures. The president of the Communications Workers of America, Glenn E. Watts, last month warned that 100,000 American jobs in the manufacture, supply and installation of telephone equipment were in danger from foreign competition, and he urged union members to begin a mail campaign to Congress asking for relief.

The layoffs and warnings of worse problems have not gone unnoticed in Washington. The Carter administration already has authorized some relief measures. For example, the President in mid-October authorized payments to laid-off steelworkers and promised more rigorous enforcement of anti-dumping laws. On Dec. 6 the administration unveiled its plan to help the steel in-

Rising Value of Imports

(in millions of dollars)

	1965	1970	1976
Passenger Cars	$ 581	$1,913	$5,451
Steel and Iron	1,140	1,952	3,809
Clothing	541	1,269	3,634
Shoes	160	629	1,686
Television Sets	60	315	833

Source: U.S. Department of Commerce

dustry, a program officials said could put between 18,000 and 35,000 steel workers back on the job *(see p. 15)*.

Some members of Congress say the administration's plan does not go far enough to protect American jobs *(see p. 17)*. Rep. Charles A. Vanik (D Ohio) has warned that if the administration does not take decisive action to reduce the pace of layoffs, Congress could pass a highly restrictive trade bill.

> One-third of Congress is isolationist [Vanik said]. They don't believe in trade. We've got 40 members whose districts are affected by textile imports, 22 by shoe imports, 19 or 20 by television imports. Add those to the 120 involved in steel, and you've got protection for everything.[2]

Even among those asking for relief from foreign competition, the demand is usually for *fair* trade rather than outright curtailment of trade. Charles Stern, president of the American Institute for Imported Steel, recently cited three basic reasons for opposing import quotas: (1) there are jobs and businesses at stake in industries which rely on imported steel; (2) quotas are likely to lead to retaliatory action by foreign countries against American exports; and (3) quotas may result in large increases in the domestic prices for steel once the moderating influence of price competition from imports is removed.[3]

Impact of '74 Recession on World Trade

Demands for protection from imports are not limited to the United States. H. Peter Dreyer, the European editor of *The Journal of Commerce,* wrote recently, "Even the most casual observer of the international trade scene cannot close his eyes to the upsurge of protectionist moves and pressures now developing in one country after another, including many which were

---

[2] Quoted in *Newsweek,* Oct. 17, 1977, p. 87.
[3] Quoted in *U.S. News & World Report,* Oct. 24, 1977, pp. 77-78.

formerly considered staunch bastions of free trade."[4] According to Wilhelm Haferkamp, vice president of the Commission of the European Communities, "The world is nearer sliding back into the protectionism of the 1930s than at any time for the last 30 years."[5]

The 1977 annual report of the International Monetary Fund noted that protectionism has been increasing in both industrialized and developing countries since the 1974-75 recession.[6] A recent study by the staff of the General Agreement on Tariffs and Trade (GATT)[7] argues that current protectionist pressures reflect a refusal to adjust to changing patterns of supply and demand, and are as much a cause as a consequence of the recent economic difficulties of the advanced economies. "By accepting the view that only a more vigorous growth of these economies will make it possible for them to return to freer trade," the authors noted, "we might be locking ourselves into a vicious circle." The report concluded that the overall stability of economies depends on their spontaneous and speedy adjustment to the inevitable constant changes in economic conditions.

Help for American Workers in '74 Act

The Trade Expansion Act of 1974 gave the United States the authority to negotiate a more liberal trade agreement with the other members of GATT. It also provided greater protection and assistance for industries and workers injured by import competition. The International Trade Commission (formerly the U.S. Tariff Commission)[8] was given the authority to recommend relief for any company or labor group able to demonstrate that it was threatened with serious losses from imports. This relief could take the form of tariffs, quotas, adjustment assistance payments *(see p. 11)* or some combination of these measures.

The act liberalized the criteria for assistance set forth in the Trade Expansion Act of 1962 *(see p. 11)*. Under the 1962 law, workers and companies had to demonstrate that they were actually suffering substantial injury from imports. The 1974 act required only that a serious threat of injury from imports be shown. In addition, the 1974 act dropped a provision from the earlier law which required that the damage to industry be caused by the removal or lowering of trade barriers.[9]

[4] H. Peter Dreyer, "International Economic Paradoxes," *European Community,* November-December 1977, p. 3.

[5] Quoted in *European Community,* November-December 1977, p. 4.

[6] International Monetary Fund, "28th Annual Report on Exchange Restrictions," 1977.

[7] Richard Blackhurst, Nicolas Marian and Jan Tumlir, "Trade Liberalization, Protectionism and Interdependence," GATT Studies in International Trade, No. 5, 1977. For more information on GATT, see p. 963.

[8] The commission advises Congress and the President on matters related to tariffs, commercial policy and foreign trade. It also investigates the impact of imports on domestic industry and agriculture.

[9] See "International Trade Negotiations," *E.R.R.,* 1976 Vol. I, pp. 343-362.

The 1974 act also redefined "dumping"—the practice of selling goods at prices below cost in foreign markets. The act broadened the ground on which a finding can be made that dumping has occurred. When such a finding has been made, the U.S. government can invoke restrictions against the offending exporter. A number of dumping complaints were filed this fall, with presidential encouragement, by the American steel industry. However, the government's new plan for aiding the industry is intended to relieve the necessity for filing complaints.

Some aspects of the 1974 trade law have proved disappointing to business and labor leaders. The procedures to be followed are lengthy and expensive, and do not necessarily result in relief. In some instances where a claim has been successful, there seems to be a tendency for the International Trade Commission to recommend less relief than the industry asked for, and for the President to grant still less.

The shoe industry, for example, filed a complaint against low-priced imports in 1975, asking for a quota system to limit the influx of foreign-made shoes. The International Trade Commission instead recommended that a combination of tariff and quota be imposed on shoe imports, but even this was rejected by President Ford. The case was reopened later in 1976 and the ITC again recommended that a tariff of 40 per cent be imposed on shoe imports exceeding 265 million pairs a year. President Carter also rejected this recommendation and instead instructed Special Trade Representative Robert S. Strauss to negotiate orderly marketing agreements with the exporting countries, a step which left control of imports partly in the exporters' hands.

Status of Current Trade Negotiations

The current round of GATT negotiations—known as the Tokyo Round[10]—has proceeded very slowly and its outcome still is in doubt. The lingering effects of the 1974-75 recession[11] have made it difficult for GATT members to reach agreement on more liberal trade rules. The dilemma facing GATT negotiators was described by H. Peter Dreyer. "On the one hand," he wrote, "governments are all aware...that in today's world their own actions must be coordinated with those of other countries, and with market situations going well beyond their individual national borders.... But against that, governments are political entities primarily responsible to their own national constituencies who will blame them (i.e. not re-elect them) if they do not cope, or at least appear to be coping, with domestic economic troubles."

---

[10] Although the current round of GATT talks began in Tokyo, the actual negotiations are being conducted at GATT headquarters in Geneva.
[11] See "World's Slow Economic Recovery," *E.R.R.* , 1977 Vol. II, pp. 745-764.

In an attempt to get the GATT talks moving, Wilhelm Haferkamp of the European Community met with U.S. Special Trade Representative Robert S. Strauss in Washington late last month. Both men reaffirmed their commitment to complete the preparatory work for the negotiations by mid-January and to then begin the actual negotiations on the final package. At a press conference for European journalists on Nov. 28, Haferkamp said he expected the negotiations to be completed by next summer.

Parallels to Past Periods

THE UNITED STATES from its earliest days imposed tariffs as a source of revenue and as a protection for fledgling industry. One of the first avowedly protectionist tariffs was passed in 1816, in response to the influx of European goods—mainly British—into the United States after the War of 1812. Protectionists—led by Henry Clay of Kentucky and John C. Calhoun of South Carolina—argued that the higher tariff would eliminate American dependence on foreign markets; consequently, American industries would flourish and a home market for surplus agricultural products would develop. "It was a matter not of procreating infant industries," wrote economist Charles P. Kindleberger, "but of preventing infanticide."[12]

U.S. tariff rates fluctuated widely during the 19th century *(see table, p. 9).* According to Kindleberger, "Tariff policy at this time was dominated by fiscal considerations. When the Treasury was pinched, as it was in 1862 during the Civil War, tariffs were raised; when revenue was ample, as in 1872, lowered."

Role of Tariffs in Onset of Depression

Parallels can be drawn between the international economic problems of today and those that prevailed after World War I. That period, too, was marked by intense competition from foreign-made goods, and the result was the same—mounting pressure for protection of American jobs. Tariff rates were raised in 1922 to the highest levels in years, thus making it difficult for the European allies to repay their war debts. It is generally agreed that the tariff policies of the 1920s contributed to the economic depression of the 1930s. As early as 1921 the *Baltimore Evening Sun* warned: "A tariff wall that keeps foreign goods out may also keep American goods in; that unless we buy from the outside we cannot sell to the outside."

---

[12] Charles P. Kindleberger, "U.S. Foreign Economic Policy, 1776-1976," *Foreign Affairs,* January 1977, p. 396. Kindleberger is Professor of Economics Emeritus at the Massachusetts Institute of Technology.

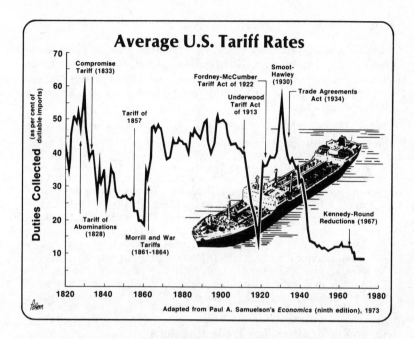

Average U.S. Tariff Rates

70 —

Compromise
Tariff (1833)

Fordney-McCumber
Tariff Act of 1922

Smoot-
Hawley
(1930)

60 —

Trade Agreements
Act (1934)

Duties Collected (as per cent of dutiable imports)

Underwood
Tariff Act
of 1913

Tariff of
1857

50 —

40 —

30 —

20 —

Tariff of
Abominations
(1828)

Kennedy-Round
Reductions (1967)

Morrill and War
Tariffs
(1861-1864)

10 —

1820   1840   1860   1880   1900   1920   1940   1960   1980

Adapted from Paul A. Samuelson's *Economics* (ninth edition), 1973

But most Americans ignored such prophets of doom. "The American people...," wrote historian Thomas A. Bailey, "did not seem to realize that a creditor nation like the United States could not expect repayment of [war] debts unless it was willing to let other nations earn the necessary dollars by exporting to it. Many Americans continued to believe that imports were basically bad."[13]

This prejudice toward imports was embodied in the Hawley-Smoot Tariff of 1930.[14] The Hawley-Smoot Tariff was, according to historians Dexter Perkins and Glyndon G. Van Deusen, "hardly more than a bundle of bargains made by the various protected interests."

> Starting out as a measure in the interest of agriculture [Perkins and Van Deusen wrote], it soon became a means of extending protection in the field of manufactures. It was another old-fashioned bill in which the interests of the consumer and of foreign trade were largely neglected.[15]

Objections to the tariff from the American Bankers Association and from industries with foreign markets were brushed aside, as was a protest by more than 1,000 American economists, mostly academicians, who addressed an appeal to President Hoover urging him to veto the bill. But Hoover, afraid a veto would

---

[13] Thomas A. Bailey, *A Diplomatic History of the American People* (1969), p. 656.
[14] A measure sponsored by Sen. Reed Smoot (R Utah) and Rep. Willis C. Hawley (R Ore.).
[15] Dexter Perkins and Glyndon G. Van Deusen, *The United States of America: A History*, Vol. II (1968), pp. 487,489.

damage the Republican Party's chances in coming congressional elections, signed the bill on June 17. The reaction to the tariff was predictable—within two years 25 countries had established retaliatory tariffs and American foreign trade took a further slump.

The Hawley-Smoot tariff greatly darkened the already gloomy international economic picture.

> Foreign exporters, unable to sell their products in America, could not build up dollar credits with which to buy American automobiles and other items.... Many nations, either for self-protection or as a reprisal, jacked up their rates or erected spite fences. Britain abandoned her historic free-trade policy, and bound the parts of her empire, including Canada, more closely to herself in imperial preference arrangements. Other nations engaged in boycotts of American goods, and in various other ways sought to quarantine the United States economically. The result was an intensification of narrow economic isolation and a worsening of that financial and political chaos which finally spawned Adolf Hitler.[16]

Movement to Liberalize Trade Relations

A turnabout in American tariff policy was inaugurated with the Reciprocal Trade Agreements Act of 1934. The movement toward lower tariffs was led by Secretary of State Cordell Hull, a Tennessean committeed to the position long popular in the South that low tariffs are good for the country. The 1934 act gave the President authority to lower tariffs on a bilateral (two-nation) basis. By incorporating "most-favored-nation" clauses in these agreements, reductions negotiated with one country would be extended to others.

By 1947, Hull and his successors had negotiated agreements with 29 nations, thereby achieving a substantial reduction on duties affecting 70 per cent of America's imports. The original act, with some modifications, was renewed by subsequent Congresses for periods ranging from one year to three years, and always in the face of considerable high-tariff Republican opposition.

After World War II the United States took the lead in trying to establish a broader approach to tariff reduction and trade liberalization. The United States proposed that an International Trade Organization (ITO) be established as part of the United Nations. This organization was to foster international economic cooperation in general and to promote freer multilateral trade in particular. The most significant work on the organization took place in Havana in 1947-48. Out of this conference evolved a charter for the proposed organization—a

---

[16] Bailey, *op. cit.,* p. 665.

charter that proved unacceptable to the U.S. government. American rejection spelled permanent defeat for the ITO.

However, before negotiations for the ITO charter were completed in 1948, a General Agreement on Tariffs and Trade (GATT) was signed in 1947 by 23 nations, including the United States. GATT was based on three cardinal principles: (1) equal, nondiscriminatory treatment for all member nations, (2) the reduction of tariffs by multilateral negotiations, and (3) the elimination of import quotas.[17]

The members of GATT have held several major negotiating rounds in the past three decades. Name designation is somewhat confusing, however. The original negotiations at Geneva in 1947, as well as subsequent bargaining sessions at Annecy, France, in 1949, at Torquay, England, in 1950-51, and again at Geneva in 1955-56, are not commonly designated by name. The Geneva session of 1960-62 is called the Dillon Round after American Secretary of the Treasury C. Douglas Dillon. The 1964-67 session is called the Kennedy Round after the President. And the current session—the Tokyo Round— carries the name of the city where it began in September 1973.

The conflicting goals of freer trade on the one hand and job protection on the other were addressed in the Trade Expansion Act of 1962. The act provided the President with broad powers to negotiate reciprocal tariff reductions. More specifically the act gave the President authority to (1) lower or eliminate entirely all tariffs on products where the Common Market countries and the United States together had 80 per cent or more of the world's trade and (2) lower tariffs up to 50 per cent on other goods over a five-year period.

Congress recognized that the sweeping tariff reductions authorized by the 1962 act would hurt some domestic industries. The act therefore provided for "trade adjustment assistance" to those who were adversely affected. Specifically, workers who lost their jobs because trade barriers were reduced could get vocational training, relocation allowances and cash payments. Adversely affected businessmen could get tax relief and loans and technical assistance for the modernization and reorganization of plants.

Achievement of the "Kennedy Round"

The Trade Expansion Act of 1962 was a major impetus for the Kennedy Round of tariff negotiations, which, after some three years of effort, were concluded at about midnight on May 15, 1967. The Kennedy Round resulted in tariff cuts on industrial

---

[17] See Campbell R. McConnell, *Economics: Principles, Problems and Policies,* 4th edition (1979), p. 738.

goods larger than any previously negotiated. About $40-billion in world trade involving some 60,000 items was made subject to tariff cuts of over one-third. The results were summarized as follows:

> The industrial countries participating in the Kennedy Round made duty reductions on 70 per cent of their dutiable imports, excluding cereals, meat and dairy products. Moreover, two-thirds of these cuts were of 50 per cent or more. Another fifth were between 25 and 50 per cent. Of the total dutiable imports on which no tariff cuts have been negotiated...one-third are subject to duties of 5 per cent or less. All this can be stated another way. Of the imports by the participating industrialized countries (other than cereals, meat and dairy products) 66 per cent are either duty free or are to be subject to cuts of 50 per cent or more.[18]

The major achievement of the Kennedy Round, according to economist Campbell R. McConnell, "was in successfully sustaining the trend toward freer trade which began over three decades ago." But McConnell added a prophetic word of caution: "Substantial tariff reductions such as those just negotiated sometimes precipitate a backlash of protectionist pressure within participating nations."[19] True to McConnell's prediction, protectionist sentiment has been rising steadily in the decade since the Kennedy Round was concluded.

Steel's Case for Protection

T HIS FALL the American steel industry became the nation's most prominent battleground in the jobs-versus-trade conflict. Bethlehem, the nation's second-largest steel manufacturer *(see box, p. 15),* incurred a third-quarter loss of $477-million, the largest ever reported by an American corporation over a three-month period. Reports of sagging profits and resulting layoffs were heard elsewhere in the industry, too. The clamor for government help, especially for import restrictions, grew louder. Americans were told that steel imports were supplying 20 per cent of the U.S. market, up from 13 per cent in the 1973-76 period. Steel's plight came to the attention of many people with great suddenness, but the situation had been years in the making.

Some observers trace steel's problems back to the 1930s when demand was so low that American steelmakers saw no reason to

---

[18] Quoted by Alan Gordon Armstrong in "The Kennedy Round," in *Britannica Book of the Year, 1968,* p. 222.
[19] McConnell, *op. cit.,* p. 741.

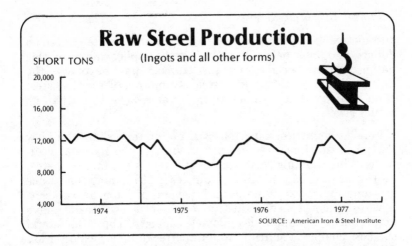

Raw Steel Production
(Ingots and all other forms)

SHORT TONS

SOURCE: American Iron & Steel Institute

modernize for efficiency, and to the 1940s and part of the 1950s when demand was so strong they saw no reason to be more efficient. While steel imports have been a growing problem for more than a decade, the dominant event of recent years was the 1974-75 world recession. Since then the global demand for steel has been sluggish. Steel production of the western industrial nations (including Japan) reached a peak of 490 million tons in the 1974 boom year and then turned downward. This year's output is expected to be about 450 million tons, and only a 5 per cent increase is forecast for 1978.[20]

In the present bear market, foreign competition has become fiercer than ever, especially in the United States, the world's foremost user of steel and steel products. The lure of the American market became doubly strong to Japanese producers after the nine member countries[21] of the European Economic Community ("Common Market") in 1975 forced Japan to limit its exports to Europe. Western Europe, though an exporter of steel, was otherwise unable to compete effectively at home against Japan's steel exports. European steelmakers face some of the same problems their American counterparts encounter—obsolete plants, outmoded equipment and wage rates higher than those in Japan. Moreover, Japanese industry is virtually strike-free, in contrast to the situation in Western Europe and America.

The European and Japanese "threat" to the American steel industry assumes an added dimension because steel is a major and basic industry. It employs 365,000 workers and its annual sales, approaching $40-billion, are surpassed only by the

[20] Figures cited by Richard J. Maloy in *European Community*, November-December 1977, p. 9. The magazine *European Community* is a publication of the European Economic Community.
[21] Britain, Belgium, Denmark, France, West Germany, Ireland, Italy, Luxembourg and the Netherlands.

automotive and petroleum industries. In addition to American dollars and jobs being at stake, steel supplies many of this nation's defense needs. Airplanes, tanks, guns, bayonets—the list of military items requiring steel is almost endless. Thus steel is an industry that assumes an importance far greater than its actual size.

Foreign countries, especially the big powers, share the view that their steelmaking capacity is vital to the national well-being. This thinking seems to be reflected in the fact that steel industries were counted in 71 countries in 1975, more than twice as many (32) as 25 years earlier. Several of the countries that have established steel industries in the last few decades have ambitions to expand or develop new capacity. Those that stand the best chance of shifting from importer to major exporter are Brazil, Mexico, Korea and Taiwan. However, the consensus of several recent studies which have attempted to forecast future steel demand and capacity is "that world wide demand for steel will fall short of supply through 1980...."[22]

"One-third of Congress is isolationist. They don't believe in trade. We've got 40 members whose districts are affected by textile imports, 22 by shoe imports, 19 or 20 by television imports. Add those to the 120 involved in steel, and you've got protection for everything."

Rep. Charles A. Vanik (D Ohio)

The American steel industry contends, and observers both in and out of government agree, that the prices at which a sizable portion of the imported steel being sold in the United States constitutes unfair competition. Typical of the industry's view was the comment by Edgar B. Speer, board chairman of the U.S. Steel Corp., that:

> American steelmakers can compete with anyone in the United States.... But when foreign producers cut their prices below cost...to keep their facilities running, U.S. companies cannot compete.[23]

With encouragement from the Carter administration, American steel companies have recently filed an unprecedented

---

[22] "Report to the President on Prices and Costs in the United States Steel Industry," the Council on Wage and Price Stability, October 1977, p. 100.
[23] Quoted in *The Washington Post*, Oct. 16, 1977.

America's Biggest Steel Companies

(1976 Statistics)

Company	Headquarters	Rank Among U.S. Industrial Concerns	Sales (in billions)	Assets (in billions)
U.S. Steel	Pittsburgh	14	$8.6	$8.8
Bethlehem	Bethlehem, Pa.	33	5.2	4.9
Armco	Middletown, Ohio	63	3.1	2.8
National	Pittsburgh	76	2.8	2.8
Republic	Cleveland	86	2.5	
Inland	Chicago	92	2.4	

Source: Fortune Directory of 500 Largest Industrial Corporations in 1976, *Fortune* magazine, May 1977, pp. 364-368

number of complaints under U.S. anti-dumping laws. However, this has been viewed a short-term measure for several reasons. The resort to dumping complaints has already evoked opposition abroad and contentions that the United States is violating international agreements. As an instrument of relief, the dumping complaint procedure is unwieldy. It takes too long, and its outcome is too uncertain to satisfy industry in the long run. Moreover, this approach does not resolve the basic problems of the steel industry.

Carter Plan for Price Reference System

President Carter called steel industry executives and labor leaders to the White House on Oct. 13 to discuss the situation. He then appointed an interagency task force, headed by Anthony M. Solomon, Under Secretary of the Treasury for Monetary Affairs, to propose a plan of action for the government to help the industry meet foreign competition and modernize itself. The task force's proposals were set out in a 35-page report to the President titled "A Comprehensive Program for the Steel Industry," released to the public on Dec. 6. They embraced a wide range of ideas, including loan guarantees and tax breaks to restore the industry's health. However, the heart of the program dealt with imports; it was a plan to curtail foreign dumping by establishing a series of "reference" prices for various categories of steel entering the United States.

These prices would be based on the costs incurred by the most efficient foreign steel producer, and would in effect be minimum prices at which steel could be sold in this country. Steel priced below these levels would automatically be subject to a prompt inquiry initiated by the government, instead of, as is now the case, by private companies. If the Treasury were to determine that steel was being sold below cost, special duties would be levied.

The precise levels at which the reference prices would be set are still under consideration. In order to gain industry acceptance of the plan, they must be set high enough to give American producers some relief from imports that are priced below cost. However, from the government's point of view, they cannot be set too high, or a number of undesirable consequences may result. Overly high prices could either shut out all significant competition and alienate the exporting countries or they could permit a general increase in steel prices which would contribute to inflation.

"Even the most casual observer of the international trade scene cannot close his eyes to the upsurge of protectionist moves and pressures now developing in one country after another, including many which were formerly considered staunch bastions of free trade."

H. Peter Dreyer in *European Community*, November-December 1977

Reference prices might cause still other problems in the months or years ahead. A reference price system might make it difficult for the steel industry to raise prices. Unless the government agreed to raise the reference prices at the same time as the industry raised prices, foreign producers would be able to expand their sales and again exert unbearable pressure on American steel companies. If the demand for steel were to remain constant or shrink further, even the degree of relief afforded by the reference price system might not be sufficient.

Proposals for Tax Cuts, Loans, Research

In attempting to enable the U.S. steel industry to survive and even prosper in a competitive world, the task force also recommended that:

The Internal Revenue Service consider tax changes to permit faster depreciation—or tax write-offs—for new machinery and equipment. This would give companies larger tax deductions and encourage modernization of obsolete facilities. Other tax advantages are expected when the administration presents a tax-reform package to Congress next year, possibly in January.

Federal loans or loan guarantees be made to assist steel companies in raising money for modernization. This part of the plan is intended to benefit companies with serious financial problems

U.S. Steel Exports and Imports

(In millions of tons)

	1973	1974	1975	1976	1977*
Imports	15.1	16	12	14.3	15.3
Exports	4.1	5.8	3	2.6	1.7

*Through October
Source: American Iron and Steel Institute

in areas of high unemployment or threatened with massive layoffs.

Assistance be provided affected steel communities by the Department of Commerce in cases where the reopening of steel plants is not practical. In addition, the task force recommended that the government study new uses for abandoned steel facilities.

The Department of Justice speed up its evaluation of requests from steel companies considering merger or a joint venture as to the department's intention in the enforcement of antitrust laws. "Some recent studies suggest that certain kinds of joint ventures in the steel industry...could reduce costs," the report said. "While the department...cannot limit or completely clarify the scope of the antitrust laws, it does have a procedure for stating in advance its enforcement intentions for proposed business conduct, including joint ventures and mergers."

Special attention be given to federal funding of research on energy conservation and pollution-abatement technology.

Environmental requirements be reviewed to see if the same goals can be attained at less cost to the steel companies. Industry sources say that current regulations make it uneconomic to modernize some facilities because the degree of efficiency to be gained would not cover the added expense of meeting anti-pollution requirements.

Freight rates be reviewed in an attempt to reduce the high cost of transporting raw materials and steel within the United States.

Establishment of a commission composed of representatives of government, industry and labor to monitor the operation of the plan, and review problems before they reach crisis proportions.

Industry and Congressional Reaction

The White House said the proposals would be put into effect by executive action—thus without requiring the consent of Congress except in the case of new tax aid. A key remaining question is that of determining how high, or low, to set the reference prices. David M. Roderick, president of U.S. Steel, suggested $360 a ton average on a wide range of steel products.

Japanese-American Trade Problems

High-level trade talks between Japan and the United States began in Washington in early December. Indications are, however, that the two sides are far apart in their proposals for improving trade relations between the two countries. Robert S. Strauss, the chief American negotiator, said the plan put forth by Nobuhiko Ushiba, Japan's Minister of External Economic Affairs, was "insufficient" and "fell considerably short of what this country...feels is necessary."

Ushiba, a former ambassador to the United States, had earlier told a news conference in Tokyo that "we will do our best to liberalize our economy." He said then that "even from the United States' point of view" the Japanese package of import-increasing measures might be considered a big one.

There are two fundamental areas in which the United States is seeking changes: (1) the elimination of high Japanese trade surpluses, and (2) the easing of Japanese restrictions on imports. Japan's trade surplus with the United States alone is expected to exceed $8-billion in 1977. Much of the recent demand for protection of U.S. industries and jobs has been a reaction to the large volume of Japanese exports to the United States.

The United States has taken some action to counteract the Japanese penetration in specific industries. The Carter administration's plan for aiding the U.S. steel industry is one example *(see p. 15)*. Another is the orderly marketing agreement on television sets negotiated last May. That agreement forestalled a recommendation by the U.S. International Trade Commission to raise tariffs on imported television sets. Under the agreement Japan agreed to sell no more than 175,000 color televisions annually in the United States, of which 190,000 would be assembled in the United States.

The other point U.S. negotiators are seeking action on is the liberalization of Japanese trade barriers. Among industrialized countries, Japan has relatively high tariffs and quotas on imports. A large proportion of Japanese imports—about 80 per cent—are food and raw materials. Manufactured goods account for the remaining 20 per cent. The United States and some European countries contend that they cannot afford to keep on buying such a large volume of Japanese manufactured goods if Japan does not make it easier for them to sell their products in Japan.

The Japanese government has difficult economic problems to resolve at home as well as in international markets. Although the Japanese economy has made substantial progress in coping with the effects of the 1974-75 recession, the Japanese economy is not as healty as the substantial trade surplus would seem to indicate. Unemployment is at its highest point in 18 years, a number of small and medium-sized companies have gone bankrupt in recent months, and the economy is growing slowly in comparison to the long-term average—about 6 per cent in the current fiscal year compared to 10.1 per cent average between 1950 and 1971.

However, a price that high is considered likely to draw heated protests from foreign steel exporters and perhaps from consumer groups at home. Higher steel prices are now considered a certainty. "And since steel price increases ripple through the economy," *The Pittsburgh Press* commented on Dec. 9, "another blip in the cost-of-living index could be in the offing."

Reaction to the task force's plan varied, but generally the industry expressed qualified approval. Armco Steel Corp., said on Dec. 8 it would not file any new dumping complaints against foreign steel companies as a sign of support for the administration's plan.

The chairman of Inland Steel Co., Frederick G. Jaicks, said on the same day that the plan, "if properly implemented, could prove to be of major significance in improving the industry's outlook for future modernization and employment stability." Some other steel executives were less enthusiastic. George A. Stenson, president of National Steel Corp., said "it will be possible to judge its effectiveness only after...six months."

Labor expressed general approval of the plan. The United Steelworkers of America issued a statement Dec. 7 calling it "a significant first step toward a necessary long-range program for developing a stronger steel industry and a stronger general economy." Among the newspaper editorial commentaries, *The Washington Post* on Dec. 7 described the plan "preferable to import quotas, which a lot of people in Congress loudly demand. As protectionist devices go, the administration's formula for reference prices is the least bad of all possibilities."

Congressional reaction tended to follow party lines, drawing praise from Democrats and criticism from Republicans. But there is no clear indication whether Carter's plan for steel will undercut the protectionist sentiment in Congress. If it does, the President may be moved to try to apply similar measures to other U.S. industries crying for help. The Carter administration obviously feels it must achieve a delicate balance between the conflicting demands of America's trading partners and its workers whose jobs become threatened by imports.

Selected Bibliography

Books

Baldwin, Robert E., *Nontariff Distortions of International Trade*, Brookings Institution, 1970.

Kindleberger, Charles P., *International Economics*, third edition, Richard D. Irwin Inc., 1963.

Piquet, Howard S., *The Trade Agreements and the National Interest*, Brookings Institution, 1958.

Samuelson, Paul A., *Economics*, ninth edition, McGraw-Hill, 1973.

Articles

Congressional Quarterly Weekly Report, Nov. 19, 1977, pp. 2467-2469.

Dreyer, H. Peter, "International Economic Paradoxes," *European Community*, November-December 1977.

"Import Restrictions on Sugar, Shoes, and TV Sets," *Regulation*, July-August, 1977.

Nehmer, Stanley, "The Promises Remain Unfulfilled: The Trade Act of 1974 Hasn't Worked," *Viewpoint*, second quarter, 1977.

"A Push for Protection," *Newsweek*, Oct. 17, 1977.

"Should U.S. Limit Steel Imports?" *U.S. News & World Report*, Oct. 24, 1977.

"Slowly from Tokyo," *The Economist*, Oct. 22, 1977.

"Testing Our Metal," *The New Republic*, Oct. 22, 1977.

"Why Steel's Dumping Cases May Backfire," *Business Week*, Nov. 14, 1977.

Will, George, "Big Steel and Big Government," *Newsweek*, Dec. 12, 1977.

Reports and Studies

Bradford, Charles A., "Japanese Steel Industry: A Comparison With Its United States Counterpart," Merrill Lynch, Pierce, Fenner & Smith, Inc., 1977.

Central Intelligence Agency, "World Steel Market: Continued Trouble Ahead," May 1977.

Council on Wage and Price Stability, "Report to the President on Prices and Costs in the United States Steel Industry," October 1977.

Editorial Research Reports, "World's Slow Economic Recovery," 1977 Vol. I, p. 747; "International Trade Negotiations," 1976 Vol. I, p. 343; "Economic Internationalism," 1973 Vol. II, p. 676.

Interagency Task Force, "Report to the President: A Comprehensive Program for the Steel Industry," Dec. 6, 1977.

International Monetary Fund, "IMF Survey," Sept. 19, 1977.

——"28th Annual Report of the International Monetary Fund," 1977.

Magee, Stephen P., "The Welfare Effects of Restrictions on U.S. Trade," Brookings Paper on Economic Activity, 1972.

Putnam, Hayes & Bartlett Inc., "Economics of International Steel Trade: Policy Implications for the United States," 1977.

WORLD'S SLOW ECONOMIC RECOVERY

by

Yorick Blumenfeld

Oct. 7
1977

WORLD'S SLOW ECONOMIC RECOVERY

THE WORLD'S recovery from the 1974-75 recession is proving to be much slower and more painful than economic experts had anticipated. Although the inflationary surge is gradually slowing down, unemployment remains at unacceptably high levels in most industrial nations and shows no indication of subsiding. Equally perturbing is the lack of any strong prospect for a significant improvement in the economic growth rates of the "locomotive" economies of the United States, West Germany and Japan during 1978. Massive balance-of-payments problems, caused largely by costly oil imports, are forcing most of the industrial countries to be far more cautious in their economic planing than in prosperous decades that preceded the recession.

The recovery tapered off quickly in many of these countries last year. This has been viewed by some experts as an indication that either the expansionary policies had been inadequate or that a quick return to the ways of economic growth was no longer as easy as in the 1960s. In the brief span of four years, two economists at the Brookings Institution have suggested, "general optimism about the outlook has been replaced by uncertainty, and assumptions about the adequacy of the international system are being questioned."[1]

The threat of another recession is viewed by Western finance ministers currently as a greater problem than inflation. Those views were expressed repeatedly at the joint annual meeting of the International Monetary Fund and the World Bank in Washington, D.C., Sept. 26-30. While the IMF in its *Annual Report,* issued two weeks before the meeting opened and based on mid-1977 conditions, saw some improvement over two years ago, it nevertheless found a "great majority" of the 131 member countries still in the process of attempting to restore order to their economies. Their problems, particularly with regard to unemployment, had brought about protectionist pressures to restrict imports. More restrictions on foreign trade, the IMF warned, will do further harm to the world's economy.

---

[1] Edward R. Fried and Philip H. Trezise, "The United States in the World Economy," *Setting National Priorities* (1976), p. 169.

This theme was echoed at the Washington meeting, where leading industrial countries were also urged to cut taxes to stimulate consumer demand. European delegates, especially, spoke approvingly of the prospect that President Carter's tax-reform package, when unveiled about mid-October, may propose $15-billion to $20-billion in tax reductions for congressional approval next year.

The United States has fared better economically than most of the world the past two years but encountered evidence of a slow-down in the summer. In August, industrial production declined for the first time since January and the national unemployment rate rose slightly to 7.1 per cent while joblessness among blacks equaled its highest peak since World War II (14.5 per cent). The nation also incurred a $2.7-billion trade deficit in August, the highest ever in one month *(see p. 27)*.

Reflecting the unease of American investors, the Dow Jones industrial average—the best-known barometer of activity on the New York Stock Exchange—closed almost daily during late September at the lowest levels since December 1975,[2] before making modest gains as the month ended. All of these factors gave rise to talk of a new recession ahead. However, this concern was eased by the government's announcement on Sept. 29 that its index of leading economic indicators had moved upward slightly in August.[3] W. Michael Blumenthal, the Secretary of the Treasury, said the news supported the Carter administration's contention that the "economy will be moving forward" toward the goal of economic growth next year that will be 5 per cent greater than the rise in inflation. Most economists predict the rate will be 4 to 5 per cent but some predictions are far lower *(see p. 26)*.

Critical Role for U.S., Japan, West Germany

Several European countries, including Britain, France, West Germany, Italy and Sweden, have slipped during the past year into what has been termed a "growth recession"—economic growth but at too slow a pace to prevent added unemployment. Speaking in Glasgow on Sept. 2, British Prime Minister James Callaghan said the economic measures agreed upon at the "Downing Street summit" in London last May by seven leading Western industrial nations[4] had not succeeded. He said that

---

[2] From a recovery high of 1014.79 on Sept. 21, 1976, "the Dow" dropped to 834.72 at the close of trading on Sept. 28, 1977. The average had fallen 10 per cent since July. See *The Wall Street Journal,* Sept. 29, 1977.

[3] Of the 10 indicators, six showed gains, three recorded minuses and one held steady. Improvement was shown in liquid assets, contracts and orders for plant and equipment, crude materials' prices, money balances, new order for consumer goods, and homebuilding permits. On the negative side were hours worked per week, slower deliveries, and stock market prices. The layoff rate remained unchanged.

[4] Britain, Canada, France, West Germany, Italy, Japan and the United States. The name comes from the Prime Minister's official residence at 10 Downing Street in London.

Real GNP Growth in Major Industrial Countries

Country	Average 1963-64 to 1973-74	From previous year		
		1975	1976	1977*
United States	4.0%	−1.8%	6.1%	5.25%
Japan	9.4	2.4	6.3	5.25
West Germany	4.4	−3.2	5.6	4.0
France	5.4	0.1	5.2	3.0
United Kingdom	2.7	−1.8	1.4	1.0
Italy	4.7	−3.5	5.6	2.25
Canada	5.4	1.1	4.9	3.0

*Annual basis for first six months
Source: OECD

neither West Germany nor the United States had been able to get the degree of expansion into their economies which they had pledged. Because the other national economies were so dependent on the leaders, Callaghan said, "We must start again."

At the London meeting, West Germany set a goal of 5 per cent economic growth this year; Japan agreed to try for 6.7 per cent and the United States set its target between 5.8 and 6 per cent. West Germany's National Institute now expects about 4 per cent growth for that country in both 1977 and 1978. Analysts for the international Organization for Economic Cooperation and Development (OECD)[5] predict the unemployment rate will rise above the 4 per cent figure, or just above one million, which is high for West Germany. Chancellor Helmut Schmidt announced on Sept. 2 that in order to hold back inflation, an upper limit of about $4-billion would be placed on next year's "pump priming" in the public sector. On the other hand, tax relief of about $3-billion is also planned in order to increase lagging domestic consumption.

Japan, another of the strong economies which had been "commissioned" to lead the Western world out of its recession, has been making an uncertain recovery. In 1976 Japan's economic growth rate accelerated to 6.3 per cent; this year it is expected to reach about 5.5 per cent, and the OECD predicts that in 1978 it may be no higher than 5 per cent. Because of sluggish domestic growth, Japan's recovery is being made through vastly increased exports.

[5] The OECD, founded in Paris in 1960 to promote economic growth among non-Communist industrial nations, today has 24 members: Australia, Austria, Britain, Belgium, Canada, Denmark, Finland, France, West Germany, Greece, Iceland, Ireland, Italy, Japan, Luxembourg, the Netherlands, New Zealand, Norway, Portugal, Spain, Sweden, Switzerland, Turkey and the United States.

Under pressure from other nations for Japan to stimulate its economy, Prime Minister Takeo Fukuda said Oct. 3 that his government would spend an additional $7.6-billion in the fiscal year ending March 31. Fukuda also told the Diet (parliament) that the country's trade surplus, an object of criticism by Japan's trading partners, would be reduced by measures now being planned. Otherwise, it might amount to $14-billion in this fiscal year.

As for the United States, the OECD estimates that real gross national product (GNP)—the sum of all goods and services—may rise 4.5 to 5 per cent in 1978. Dr. Alice Rivlin, director of the Congressional Budget Office, has predicted that real growth would slow down and that only fairly modest improvements would be made in inflation and unemployment rates in the months ahead. The Joint Economic Committee of Congress, in a mid-year 1977 report issued on Sept. 25, called the outlook "unfavorable" through the rest of the year and well into 1978—an appraisal about as pessimistic as Dr. Rivlin's.

Among non-government economists, a panel of nine of the nation's best-known private economists, brought together recently by *Time* magazine for their views, forecast growth in the 4.5 to 5 per cent range through the middle of next year.[6] In contrast, Michael Evans, head of Chase Econometrics Associates, anticipates real GNP at no more than 3 per cent for the rest of this year and 1.6 per cent for all of next year.

Carter has called for a White House conference early next year on "Balanced National Growth and Economic Development." Clearly he is concerned about stemming any further loss of confidence in the economy. Indeed, the OECD has pointed out that "gradualism" in the American economy can pose problems abroad. While the President obviously would like to fulfill his election pledge[7] to reduce inflation and unemployment while balancing the federal budget by 1981, the rest of the world is hoping that the administration will "reflate" the economy through further increases in public spending.

Slow Growth of Trade; America's Big Deficit

Although the volume of world trade this year is likely to rise between 5 and 6 per cent, according to Britain's National Institute, this compares with an average annual growth in world trade of 7 per cent in the years 1965-1975 and of 12 per cent in

[6] "Recovery on a Tightrope," *Time*, Oct. 3, 1977, pp. 75-77. The magazine noted many differences of opinion between "conservative" (Alan Greenspan, Murray Weidenbaum, Beryl Sprinkel) and the "more liberal members" of the panel (Walter Heller, David Grove, Robert Nathan, Arthur Okun, Joseph Pechman). The remaining member, Otto Eckstein, was not classified as liberal or conservative.

[7] Carter's specific targets for 1981 are to reduce unemployment to 4.67 per cent, inflation to 4.3 per cent and balance the federal budget, holding expenditure and revenue levels to no more than 21 per cent of GNP.

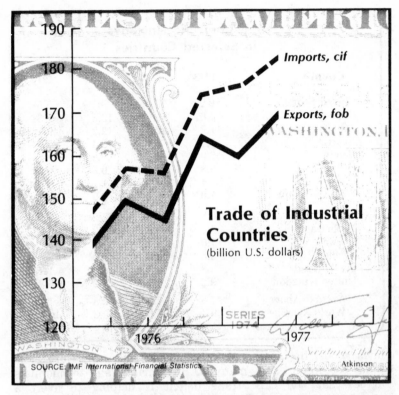

Trade of Industrial Countries
(billion U.S. dollars)

Imports, cif

Exports, fob

190
180
170
160
150
140
130
120

1976   1977

SOURCE: IMF *International Financial Statistics*   Atkinson

1976.[8] Recent data compiled by the IMF indicate that the growth of global trade is shrinking after reaching the $1-trillion level last year. Economists note that without the increase in oil shipments, world trade this year would have risen only about 4 per cent.

American imports, led by oil, have been running nearly 20 per cent above those of 1976 and, as a consequence, the U.S. trade balance has been registering record monthly deficits, reaching a high so far of $2.7-billion in August. Treasury Secretary Blumenthal told a news conference on Sept. 27 that the year-end trade deficit was likely to approach $30-billion, four times higher than the previous record deficit of $6.4-billion in 1972. Economists seemed to be evenly divided between those who believe the trade deficits will cause trouble unless quickly reduced and those who believe that the remedy will cause even worse difficulties.

The main reason for the trade gap, aside from America's increasing dependence on foreign oil, is that the U.S. economy has been growing faster than those of its principal trading partners. As a result, imports have risen sharply and exports have not kept pace, even though a big item in America's export trade,

[8] The National Institute, *Economic Review 1976-77*, p. 4.

Consumer Price Increases in Selected Countries

Country	1973	1974	1975	1976
United States	6.2%	11.0%	9.1%	5.5%
Canada	7.6	10.9	10.8	7.6
Japan	11.7	22.7	12.2	9.7
Austria	7.5	9.5	8.4	7.3
Belgium	7.0	12.6	12.8	9.2
Denmark	9.3	15.3	9.8	9.0
France	7.4	13.6	11.8	9.6
West Germany	7.0	7.0	5.9	4.6
Italy	10.8	19.1	17.2	15.7
Netherlands	8.1	9.6	10.2	8.8
Norway	7.5	9.4	11.7	9.2
Sweden	6.8	9.8	9.9	10.4
Switzerland	8.8	9.8	6.8	1.7
United Kingdom	9.2	15.9	24.2	16.8
Average Above	7.5	12.6	10.8	7.7
World Average	9.4	15.0	13.3	10.7

Source: IMF *International Financial Statistics*, September 1977

farm goods, has remained strong so far this year. Europeans tend to argue—and many U.S. officials and economists agree—that the U.S. trade deficit is helping to avert a worldwide recession. But others argue that this country is shouldering too much of the burden. Moreover, they contend that enormous trade deficits will further weaken the value of the dollar abroad and consequently create instability in the world money markets.

West Germany, which had a favorable balance of trade of $13.7-billion last year, is expected to have a more modest surplus of $2.5-billion when 1977 ends. However, France is likely to record a deficit of about $4.5-billion, Canada about $4-billion, and 10 other OECD countries together will show deficits of $12-billion, according to recent projections. Last year these 12 countries borrowed more than $14-billion to help finance their oil imports.

Inflation's Persistence in the Industrial West

Although inflation varies widely from country to country, the overall rate for the 24 OECD nations during the second half of 1976 was about 8 per cent. Emile van Lennep, the organization's Secretary General, suggests there is little prospect of bringing it below that level in the near future.[9] However, falling prices of such basic commodities as sugar, grain and vegetable oils will help keep inflation from advancing even faster.

[9] Emile van Lennep, "The Growth Strategy in the Present Economic Context," *OECD Observer*, May 1977, p. 3.

Geoffrey H. Moore wrote in the August issue of the *Morgan Guaranty Survey,* the New York bank's monthly newsletter, that "once inflation gets going, it tends to keep going." There is natural motion to inflation, with wages and prices chasing each other. Moreover, inflation benefits certain groups or individuals. "Those whose incomes rise faster than the cost of living are the winners," Leonard Silk observed in *The New York Times.*[10] Weak, minority governments in Western Europe have proved themselves unable to restrain the wage demands of powerful labor unions.

American economists appear to agree that the U.S. inflation rate may be held to 6 per cent in 1978. However, it is expected to stay above 10 per cent in Australia, Britain, Denmark, Finland, France, Ireland, Italy and Sweden. All efforts to stabilize prices in Britain and other OECD countries involve a short-run trade-off between unemployment and inflation. In many countries, according to international trade specialists in Geneva, stopping inflation has meant budget tightening and subsequent joblessness.[11]

Dilemma Over Reducing High Unemployment

Most OECD member countries are faced with the likelihood of higher unemployment in the coming year. There are already over 15 million people out of work in the Western industrial nations, including almost seven million in the United States. Unemployment levels vary between 4 and 6 per cent in Europe, and range above 7 per cent in the United States and 8 per cent in Canada. It is estimated that between 30 and 40 per cent of the unemployed are under age 25.

President Valery Giscard d'Estaing recently termed youth unemployment the "No. 1 national priority" in France. Following the London summit meeting in May, the seven national leaders issued a statement saying: "Our most urgent task is to create more jobs while continuing to reduce inflation.... We are particularly concerned about the problem of unemployment among young people. We have agreed that there will be an exchange of experience and ideas on providing the young with job opportunities."

The National Institute of Economic and Social Research in London has urged the British government to reflate the economy or face the prospect of adding 300,000 members to the already swollen ranks of the unemployed. The British, with 1.4 million persons out of work, are beginning to worry that high unemployment may once again become a permanent fixture.

---

[10] June 16, 1977.
[11] General Agreement on Tariffs and Trade, *GATT Report for 1975-76,* p. 17.

"Long periods of unemployment will be the lot of many," *The Times* of London said editorially, "and as the years go by it will become obvious that this affects all age groups." Britain's job-creation program has so far provided about 100,000 temporary jobs at a cost of about $250-million, while 200,000 other jobs are being supported by temporary employment subsidies.

American sociologist Daniel Bell writes, "If one searches for a solution, the double bind manifests itself in the fact that inflation or unemployment have become virtual tradeoffs of government policy, and governments are in the difficult position of constantly redefining what is an 'acceptable' level of unemployment and an 'acceptable' level of inflation."[12] For countries facing a "parliamentary impasse"—and there is not a single majority government in Western Europe—this dilemma is becoming increasingly painful.

Background of Current Impasse

T HE PROSPERITY that followed World War II in the industrial West lasted for a quarter of a century with only brief interruptions in one country or another. It was long enough for many people to forget that prolonged periods of favorable economic conditions have, historically, been the exception rather than the norm. The expansive economic theories of John Maynard Keynes held sway, and it became popular to regard business slumps as products of outmoded thinking.

The postwar boom lasted until 1974, when national economies throughout the world were suddenly hit by the devastating effects of oil prices that had been doubled and doubled again during the previous fall and winter by the Organization of Petroleum Exporting Countries (OPEC).[13] There were other causes, to be sure, for most of the industrial nations were suffering some forms of economic weakness, but none carried such force as the sudden surge in expenditures for oil.

Analysts have been busy studying not only the loss of prosperity but the factors that created the prosperity in the first place. The OECD attributes the postwar boom to rapid and widespread technological progress, the need for reconstruction of war-ravaged areas, stable supplies of low-priced raw materials and energy, and a favorable political and economic climate created by governments. An OECD study, put together

---

[12] Daniel Bell, "The Future World Disorder," *Foreign Policy*, summer 1977, p. 119.
[13] Current members are Algeria, Ecuador, Gabon, Iran, Iraq, Indonesia, Kuwait, Libya, Nigeria, Qatar, Saudi Arabia, United Arab Emirates and Venezuela.

by eight independent economists headed by Paul McCracken, said that the potential for rapid growth could not have been realized had the Western governments not been committed to economic integration in the framework of an open multilateral system for international trade payments.[14]

No feature of this boom, which is already becoming known as an "economic golden age," was more remarkable than the expansion of world trade. From 1953 to 1973 the volume of trade grew by an average of 8 per cent a year. The world's gross domestic product increased by more than three and a half times. Moreover, unemployment was at historically low levels in most countries throughout this period.

It has been suggested that economists thought governments could control upswings and downswings in national income by maintaining a high level of demand and thus preventing upheavals in trade, prices, production and employment which had recurred in the past. Moreover, almost every Western society manipulated part of the economy through deficit financing, as expounded by Keynes. In the United States the failure to finance the war in Vietnam adequately through taxes after 1965, as well as the added demands brought on by President Johnson's Great Society program, led to an inflationary spiral.

At the end of the 1960s, most industrial economies experienced recurrent periods in which wages rose faster than productivity and price trends would warrant. In an effort to control the inflationary tide in the United States, the Federal Reserve Board began imposing higher interest rates and other economic restraints. But the attempts to maintain the parity of the dollar in the face of years of deteriorating competitiveness led to a massive balance-of-payments deficit, an overly rapid increase in liquidity elsewhere, and ultimately the breakdown of the world monetary system which had been established in Bretton Woods, N.H., in 1944.[15]

Shocks Following 1973 Oil-Price Increases

A number of economic factors led to the recession that hit the world in 1974. First, there was an extraordinary rate of monetary expansion in most countries following the economic slowdown of 1970-1971. In those two years official reserves in the OECD countries increased by a third. A speculative crisis culminated in June 1972 with the floating of sterling and the temporary closing of exchange markets as devaluation rumors spread to the dollar and the Italian lira. The monetary expansion accounted

---

[14] Paul McCracken et al., "Towards Full Employment and Price Stability," OECD, June 1977, p. 11. McCracken was head of the Council of Economic Advisers during the Nixon presidency.

[15] See "Economic Internationalism," *E.R.R.*, 1973 Vol. II, pp. 676-677.

for the typically speculative features of a subsequent boom. The price of gold and real estate soared. Speculation in commodities, superimposed on a sequence of agricultural harvest failures, upset the markets.

The biggest shock to the international economic system was imparted by the quadrupling of the price of oil in the fall of 1973 and the following winter. This brought on a new round of inflation and magnified existing faults in the world monetary structure. To counter the threat of runaway inflation, virtually all of the OECD countries imposed restrictive trade practices. And these practices swiftly brought on a recession. Total world production declined for the first time since the 1930s. Many of the less-developed countries were saved from bankruptcy only by massive borrowing; even the countries of Western Europe ran up large debts.

Unsettling Effect of Surplus Petroleum Funds

The billions of oil revenues that OPEC was amassing also exercised a contractional effect. The oil-exporting states increased their surpluses, even after vastly heavier spending, from just $5-billion in 1973 to more than $44-billion in 1976. To the extent that this surplus money was, and continues to be, used to acquire property and other existing assets in the West, the effect was to take spending power out of the world's economic system without putting anything back in its place.

Although the OECD states managed to increase their exports to the oil-producing countries more rapidly than had been expected—in large part through the increased export of arms—"recycling petro-dollars" became an important economic issue.[16] For example, *Business Week* reported last spring that the world's principal oil exporter, Saudi Arabia, was running out of banks in which it could safely deposit its growing surplus of funds. Even with billions of dollars invested in long-term securities in the United States, Britain, Switzerland, West Germany and Japan, the Saudis are still seeking more outlets for their accumulating treasure.

The need for adjustment between the surplus and deficit countries consequently remains a pressing issue. George Williams, director general of the United Kingdom Offshore Operators Association, predicted in August that world oil prices will double by 1985. Even if the prices remain unchanged, oil-importing nations still face huge deficits in the years ahead. Secretary General van Lennep has written: "Whereas previously it was expected that the oil bill of the OECD countries would start declining at constant prices in the last years of this decade,

---

[16] See "Arab Oil Money," *E.R.R.*, 1974 Vol. I, p. 365.

the current projections suggest a further $20-billion increase between 1977 and 1980 at today's prices."[17]

The world economic recovery that began in 1975 was presumed to be long-lasting. Accordingly, the governments of the industrial countries were intentionally cautious about the rates at which they reflated their economies. Experience had shown them that, when their economies were abruptly turned about, new inflationary trends arose and localized shortages occurred. This caution, however, did not build business confidence. The result was that investment in new plant and equipment was insufficient to lower the rates of unemployment. Investment in manufacturing, together with a rise in exports, was the chief goal of most national recovery plans.

Many European manufacturers have refused to invest because of the difficulties in borrowing at high interest rates and because of a lower level of current sales and profits. The problems for the economy have thus been aggravated by the fact that the cost of labor and materials has continued at a very high level relative to prices. Much of the new investment in industry has consequently been directed at saving labor and reducing costs rather than expanding capacity and providing new jobs. The ratio of after-tax profits to equity in Britain in 1975 was 0.7 per cent and in the United States was 3.5 per cent. A decade earlier, the return on equity in the United States had averaged 13.1 per cent. Such low returns were yet another disincentive to the troubled world economies.

Outlook for Return to Prosperity

T HE OIL crisis of 1973 pointed forcibly to the fact that national economies are interrelated. The Club of Rome wrote in 1974 of the futility of trying to solve crises "in isolation...at the expense of others." "Real solutions are apparently interdependent; collectively, the whole multitude of crises appears to constitute a single global crisis-syndrome of world development."[18]

Because of such global synchronization, hopes for recovery in the industrial world have rested heavily on American, German and Japanese shoulders. The cautious, pragmatic and non-doctrinaire approach of the Carter administration in inter-

---

[17] Emile van Lennep and Ulf Lantzke, "The World Energy Outlook for the Next Ten Years," *OECD Observer*, March 1977, p. 5.

[18] Mihajlo Mesarovic and Eduard Pestel, *Mankind at the Turning Point* (1974), The Second Report to the Club of Rome, p. 1.

national economic affairs has not been helpful in this respect, Frank Vogl of *The Times* of London wrote on Aug. 2. Washington has not demonstrated enthusiasm "for any form of deep and detailed policy planning [that exists] between most industrialized nations," Vogl said. The OECD report "Towards Full Employment and Price Stability" said the world is moving toward a market-oriented "federative" system which requires "better international coordination of demand management policies."

Efforts to Expand Trade and Reduce Barriers

Although the world economies became adjusted to the vigorous expansion of trade during the 1948-73 era, doubts have arisen over whether even moderate trade expansion is in prospect for the remaining years of this decade. Economist Gordon Tether, writing July 10 in *The Observer* of London, pointed out that there is a widespread tendency among people in the industrial nations to finance leisure activities and forego much of their spending on items that were formerly considered essential such as clothing or consumer durables. This change in spending habits is not fully reflected in production. Some markets are saturated while others are not adequately serviced.

The average tariffs imposed by the major industrial nations today are less than 10 per cent of the goods' value, a fraction of the early postwar levels. However, the dangers of a worldwide drift back to protectionist trade policies are considered greater today than when ministerial-level officials representing nearly 100 nations met in Tokyo in 1973 and agreed to open negotiations aimed at making international trade freer.[19]

The IMF, for example, reported increased use of protectionist trade measures both last year and this year. Import restrictions include non-tariff barriers to trade "applied on a selective basis" by various countries and "negotiated" export-restraint agreements on items ranging from Japanese television sets to shoes from Taiwan or textiles from Korea. Such restrictions were the result of intensified pressures on governments to protect weak domestic industries from foreign competition and thus preserve jobs, while simultaneously boosting exports and employment by subsidies.

With the growth of commodity cartels,[20] preferential markets, and other protectionist measures, Wilhelm Haferkamp, the European Common Market's minister for external affairs, warned last summer against "seductive modern, rational-

---

[19] Thus began the "Tokyo Round" of trade negotiations, under auspices of the General Agreement on Tariffs and Trade (GATT). Negotiations have since been conducted in Geneva.

[20] See "International Cartels," *E.R.R.*, 1974 Vol. II, pp. 343-362.

sounding slogans of protectionism." In a speech to the French Chamber of Commerce in the United States in July, Prime Minister Raymond Barre cautioned that "the liberalism which inspired trade negotiations in the 1960s will not insure the peaceful growth of trade in today's world."

Barre suggested "organizing free trade" to "permit a harmonious international sharing of economic activity and to avoid the double danger of ruinous competition...and the emergence of national monopolies." Laurence Krauss, a senior fellow at the Brookings Institution, characterized Barre's plan as "a scheme to cartelize world trade." However, French officials countered that most Western industrial nations were preaching free trade while increasing their trade restrictions.

"In a period where pressures are developing for a return to protectionism, it is essential for the main trading nations to...avoid...measures by which they could solve their problems at the expense of others...."

From the Declaration of Rambouillet
Nov. 17, 1975, by leaders of six
leading industrial nations

Alonzo McDonald, the new U.S. ambassador to the General Agreement on Tariffs and Trade, arrived in Geneva on Sept. 6 to work toward completion of the preliminary phase of new agreements by Jan. 15, 1978, and full agreement by the end of next year. Formal talks on tariff formulas and trade agreements are scheduled to start in January. Economist Melvyn Westlake, writing in *The Times* of London, said it would be "optimistic to expect further tariff cuts of more than a quarter on average." This would be only half of what was achieved during the Kennedy Round[21] of tariff cuts in the mid-1960s.

Pacts for Controlling Commodity Fluctuations

The current round of negotiations on commodity agreements stems from the harmful effects of wide fluctuations in prices over the past four years. Although the OECD considers "generalized government interference in commodity markets" an inefficient means of regulation, the "boom and bust" cycle of such commodities as coffee, sugar, tin and cereals benefits only the speculators. The IMF reported in September that its com-

---

[21] Named for President Kennedy, who initiated these trade talks under GATT sponsorship in 1962.

posite price index of 37 basic commodities fell 14.5 per cent from April to July, the latest month for which statistics had been compiled. Wheat, for example, which was selling at about $5 a bushel a few years ago, is now down to about $2 a bushel because of a mounting world surplus.[22]

High wheat prices were an important factor in the general upward thrust of commodity prices in 1972-1974 and contributed to the world inflationary spiral. Now grain-consuming nations are upset that just before the next round of talks between producers and consumers to renegotiate the International Wheat Agreement, the Carter administration on Aug. 29 ordered a 20 per cent cut in wheat acreage to prevent a further fall in prices. In announcing the new policy, Deputy Secretary of Agriculture John C. White proposed a new international grain reserve to aid "the fight against world hunger."

It was estimated that a 20 per cent cut would reduce the U.S. wheat crop next year by about 20 million tons. It seemed anomalous that while America opposed export restrictions and production cuts by other nations, it was willing to apply such measures when it sought to protect its interest as a producer. Officials in the U.S. Department of Agriculture countered that the United States should not be seen forever as the world's bread basket and that these acreage cuts could be an important incentive to developing countries to step up their own output.

Gamani Corea, Secretary General of the U.N. Conference on Trade and Development (UNCTAD), complained in a report last July that the talks on a proposed integrated program for stabilizing world commodity prices was falling behind schedule. Of the eight commodities discussed in the preceding six months, there had been a "detailed and constructive dialogue" only on rubber. The position of the United States appeared to be a barrier, according to a number of delegates. Bolivia, for example, complained of Washington's refusal to accept higher prices for tin under the International Tin Agreement. Technical problems, still being debated, may bar a solution at UNCTAD's next meeting in Geneva in November.

IMF Attempts to Ease Poor Nations' Debt

In a world that is increasingly interdependent economically, the trauma of developing nations that lack oil resources is a major concern. Henry C. Wallich, a governor of the U.S. Federal Reserve System, said recently that total claims by commercial banks on countries other than the Group of Ten[23] leading industrial nations had soared to $193-billion at the end of March

---

[22] See "International Financial Statistics" of the IMF, September 1977.

[23] Belgium, Britain, Canada, France, West Germany, Italy, Japan, the Netherlands, Sweden and the United States.

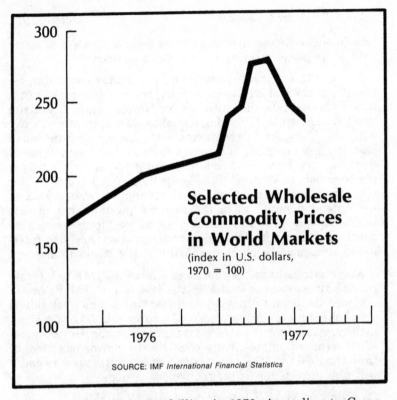

Selected Wholesale Commodity Prices in World Markets

(index in U.S. dollars, 1970 = 100)

300

250

200

150

100

1976   1977

SOURCE: IMF *International Financial Statistics*

1977—up from about $75-billion in 1972. According to Corea, the debt of developing countries alone will reach $253-billion by the end of 1978.

Such a vast debt structure poses tremendous strains on the world economy. Debt servicing alone is expected to absorb 25 per cent of the export earnings of the developing countries next year. Economists at Morgan Guaranty Trust of New York estimate that the amount of maturing debt of these countries is also climbing rapidly. Last year they had only $12-billion to repay but it is estimated that $18-billion will fall due next year.

At the Conference on International Economic Cooperation in Paris in May, the foreign ministers of 27 rich and poor nations issued a communiqué after two days of bargaining which acknowledged the two groups could not reach an agreement on various aspects of external indebtedness. The poor countries were reported to be dismayed that the rich were unwilling to commit themselves to 0.7 per cent of their GNP for development aid by 1980.[24] Suggestions for a moratorium on the debts of the poorest countries, now estimated at about $40-billion, were also rebuffed. Finance ministers of more than 100 countries are

[24] See *The Economist,* June 4, 1977, p. 97.

scheduled to discuss the increasingly serious problem of world debt at a special meeting in Geneva in January.

Much of this borrowing has been from commercial banks, especially in the United States, and has resulted in criticism that they have overextended their credit. Harold van B. Cleveland and Bruce Brittain, U.S. commercial bankers currently on leave with the Bank for International Settlements, have defended past lending practices and regard "the extraordinary surge of demand" for loans to developing countries as "a temporary phenomenon." Writing in *Foreign Affairs* in July 1977, Cleveland and Brittain criticized economists who, afraid of widespread defaults, take the extreme position that private banks should withdraw entirely from long-term lending to developing countries and leave that function solely to international agencies such as the IMF and the World Bank.

Major efforts have been made to enable the IMF to increase its effectiveness as a lender of the last resort. The Fund announced the conditions Aug. 30 under which a new $10-billion supplementary financing "facility" is to operate. The Witteveen facility, named for the IMF's managing director, Dr. Johannes Witteveen, will enable many countries to borrow more money from the IMF than their quotas currently entitle them to and it will also provide for longer repayment periods.

Question of Making Interdependence Workable

The world economies have suffered severe dislocations while the member governments have tried to puzzle their way out of the slump. Professor Ralf Dahrendorf, director of the London School of Economics, suggests that the West may be

Global Structure of Current Account Balances*

(in billions of U.S. dollars)

Groupings	Average 1967-72	1973	1974	1975	1976	Projections 1977
Major oil-exporting countries	0.7	6	67	35	41	37
Industrial countries	10.2	12	−10	19	−1	−1
Other non-oil countries						
More developed	−1.7	1	−14	−12	−14	−12
Less developed	−8.1	−11	−30	−38	−26	−25
Total	1.1	8	−14			−1

*On goods, services and private transfers

SOURCE: IMF, *1977 Annual Report*

approaching the end of the social-liberal consensus which has governed its politics since the end of World War II. The "twin goals of an incentive approach to economic growth and public welfare for all are no longer compatible," he said.[25] The British ambassador to the United States, Peter Jay, writes in *The Future That Doesn't Work* that because Western governments are politically committed to full employment, they cannot take the inflation-curbing steps necessary to guarantee economic stability.

Making interdependence a more workable proposition in a world of proud, sovereign states remains one of the core problems. Daniel Bell suggests that economic nationalism could lead some of the poor and weak governments to invoke "import restrictions because they fear to impose socially disastrous and politically dangerous austerity measures at home." The consequence, Bell fears, may be a further period of international recession.

The world obviously needs to build or perfect cooperative mechanisms to stabilize commodity markets, determine beneficial levels of growth and regulate the monetary systems in ways which would lead to sustained full employment and price stability. In order to build such genuine foundations for the future, economists agree that what the world needs most right now is a long and peaceful period of steady expansion of both production and trade.

---

[25] Writing in *The Wall Street Journal,* Aug. 18, 1977.

Selected Bibliography

Books

Hirsch, Fred, *Money International,* Allen Lane, 1967.
Johnson, Harry G., *Trade Strategy,* George Allen and Unwin, 1971.
Mesarovic, Mihajlo and Pestel, Eduard, *Mankind at the Turning Point,* The Second Report to the Club of Rome, Hutchinson, 1974.
Odell, Peter R., *Oil and World Power,* Penguin, 1975.
Owen, Henry and Schultze, Charles L., *Setting National Priorities,* The Brookings Institution, 1976.

Articles

Amuzegar, Jahangir, "A Requiem for the North-South Conference, *Foreign Affairs,* October 1977.
Bell, Daniel, "The Future World Disorder," *Foreign Policy,* summer 1977.
Cleveland, Harold van B., and W.H. Bruce Brittain, "Are the LDC's in Over Their Heads," *Foreign Affairs,* July 1977.
"The IMF Wields Sudden New Power, *Business Week,* March 28, 1977.
Moore, Geoffrey H., "Five Little Known Facts About Inflation," *Morgan Guaranty Survey,* August 1977.
"The North and South Are Still on Speaking Terms—Just," *The Economist,* June 4, 1977.
The *OECD Observer,* selected issues 1976-77.
Palmer, Rita, "A Row Over Trade," *Newsweek,* International edition, Aug. 22, 1977.
"Rich Countries Getting Poorer," *Economist,* Sept. 10, 1977.

Reports and Studies

Cooper, Richard N. and Lawrence, Robert Z. "The 1972-1975 Commodity Boom," Brookings Papers on Economic Activity, 1975.
Editorial Research Reports, "International Trade Negotiations," 1976 Vol. I, p. 343; "World Financing Under Stress," 1975 Vol. I, p. 287; "Economic Internationalism," 1973 Vol. II, p. 676.
Haberler, Gottfried, "Incomes Policy and Inflation: An Analysis of Basic Principles," American Enterprise Institute for Public Policy Research, 1977.
"International Financial Statistics," International Monetary Fund, September 1977.
"International Trade 1975-76," General Agreement on Tariffs and Trade, Geneva, 1976.
Paul McCracken, et al., "Towards Full Employment and Price Stability," an OECD report, June 1977.
Whitman, Marina v. N., "Coordination and Management of the International Economy: A Search for Organizing Principles" in *Contemporary Economic Problems,* William Fellner, ed., American Enterprise Institute for Public Policy Research, 1977.

WELFARE IN AMERICA AND EUROPE

by

Mary Costello

**Dec. 9
1977**

WELFARE IN AMERICA AND EUROPE

A MERICANS tend to view the idea of the welfare state with something approaching horror. Western Europeans, on the other hand, typically regard it as a necessity, a civilized, albeit costly, way of redistributing income to eliminate dire poverty. The so-called "cradle-to-grave security" systems in effect in Scandinavia, the Low Countries and Britain have succeeded to a large extent in providing a basic level of subsistence for all. Yet, the taxpayers have paid a high price for these programs.

Concern about the cost of social welfare programs in those countries has provoked a public outcry, particularly in Britain,[1] about welfare "chiselers" and has led to demands that something be done to halt the rapid expansion of these programs. While there have been numerous proposals for making the systems more efficient and subsequently less costly, it is unlikely that any country will dismantle its cradle-to-grave security programs in the near future. The European attachment to existing systems was expressed by Dr. Elizabeth Weiser of Austria's Ministry of Social Welfare. She told a Canadian journalist: "I accept that the state owes a minimum duty to its people. We don't want to go the way of the Americans."[2]

The American welfare system is often described as chaotic, unmanageable, inefficient, inequitable, riddled with fraud, degrading to those it is intended to help and increasingly burdensome on those who pay for it. Through the years, there have been countless attempts to reform the so-called "welfare mess." The latest effort was outlined by President Carter on Aug. 6 and legislation was introduced in Congress Sept. 12. Amid considerable opposition, the House Welfare Reform Subcommittee has begun marking up the bill and expects to finish by early January.[3] The Senate Finance Committee, preoccupied with energy and social security legislation, has not yet taken any action on the bill.

---

[1] See *The Future That Doesn't Work: Social Democracy's Failures in Britain* (1977) by E. Emmett Tyrell Jr. See also "Britain: Debtor Nation," *E.R.R.,* 1977 Vol. II, pp. 255-256.
[2] Quoted by Walter Stewart, "The God That Failed," *Maclean's,* Jan. 24, 1977, p. 34.
[3] The subcommittee was set up specifically to study the Carter welfare proposal. It is composed of members from three permanent committees—Ways and Means, Agriculture, and Education and Labor—and is under the chairmanship of Rep. James C. Corman (D Calif.).

The administration's proposal, called the Program for Better Jobs and Income, would, the President said, "transform the manner in which the federal government deals with the income needs of the poor and begin to break the welfare cycle" by providing jobs for those who need work, dispensing fairer and more uniform cash benefits, promoting family stability and improving the self-respect of recipients. It would abolish three key elements of the existing welfare system: (1) Aid to Families with Dependent Children (AFDC), (2) Supplementary Security Income (SSI) for the blind, aged and disabled and (3) food stamps. About 30 million persons receive assistance under these programs. Carter would replace their benefits with cash grants. Medicaid, which pays part or all of the medical expenses of 24.7 million people and costs $17.2-billion a year, was not dealt with in the Carter program since the administration expects a national health insurance plan to be enacted to cover the medical expenses of the poor.

Carter's Plan for Better Jobs and Income

Carter explained that his welfare proposal consists of a "job-oriented program for those able to work and a simplified, uniform, equitable cash assistance program for those in need who are unable to work by virtue of disability, age or family circumstances." Cash benefits for Americans able but unwilling to work would be reduced. Up to 1.4 million full- and part-time public service jobs would be created for persons unable to find employment elsewhere. These jobs would pay the federal minimum wage[4] and recipients would be required to spend five weeks each year looking for non-subsidized employment. The Program for Better Jobs and Income, Carter said, "will ensure that work will always be more profitable than welfare and that a private or non-subsidized public job will always be more profitable than a special federally funded public service job."

The work requirements have been criticized by the Congressional Black Caucus, the National Association of Social Workers and many liberals, among others, but they may be necessary to ensure passage of any welfare proposal. A public opinion poll conducted last summer by *The New York Times* and CBS News showed that 58 per cent of the respondents disapproved of "most government-sponsored welfare programs"; only 31 per cent approved. Some 54 per cent concurred with the statement that "most people who receive money from welfare could get along without it if they tried." However, the antagonism toward the concept of welfare was not reflected in the answers to questions about helping the needy. Eighty-one per cent of those questioned approved of food stamps for the poor

---

[4] Currently $2.30 an hour and $2.65 beginning Jan. 1, 1978.

Major Income Assistance Programs

Program	Date Enacted	Recipients* (millions)	Fiscal Year 1977 Expenditures** (billions)	
			State & Local	Federal
General Assistance	N.A.	0.9	$ 1.3	$ 0.0
Veterans Pensions	1933	2.3	0.0	3.1
Aid the Families with Dependent Children	1935	11.4	4.6	5.7
Housing Assistance	1937	3.0	N.A.	3.0
Food Stamps	1964	17.7	N.A.	5.0
Medicaid	1965	24.7	7.5	9.7
Basic Opportunity Grants	1972	1.9	0.0	1.8
Supplemental Security Income	1972	4.4	1.6	4.7
Earned Income Tax Credit	1975	6.3	0.0	1.3
Total			$15.0	$34.3
Total (Federal, state and local)				$49.3

* The total number of recipients is not the sum of the recipients of each program, because many persons receive benefits from more than one program.
** Estimates

Source: *The Budget of the United States Government, Fiscal Year 1978*, January 1977

and aid to poor families with dependent children; 82 per cent favored free health care for people unable to afford it.

The Carter proposal, like a similar plan offered by President Nixon in 1969 called the Family Assistance Plan (FAP), takes this ambivalence into consideration. Robert Lekachman, the economist, described the Carter plan as an effort to "reconcile mild altruism toward the poor, strong Protestant inclinations to set the idle to useful labor, ideological preferences for the private over the public sector, a consuming urge by the end of the first Carter administration to seize the Holy Grail of a balanced national budget and the political necessity to ward off the damaging assaults from the left and right which defeated FAP."[5]

The author of Nixon's Family Assistance Plan was Daniel Patrick Moynihan, now a Democratic senator from New York. Moynihan initially praised the Carter plan as "magnificent and superbly crafted," describing it as "the most important piece of social legislation since the New Deal." But in testimony before

---

[5] Robert Lekachman, "The Welfare Mess: Carter's Reforms Make Sense for Some, but the Cities Lose Again," *Politicks & Other Human Interests*, Nov. 22, 1977, p. 18. Lekachman, Distinguished Professor of Economics at Lehman College, City University of New York, is the author of *Economists at Bay* (1975).

the House Welfare Reform Subcommittee on Sept. 30, he called it "grievously disappointing" and warned that it would not "attract the necessary coalition of support."

Both the Carter and Nixon plans avoided the kind of reform that would bring the American system into line with the so-called "welfare states" in Europe. Robert Reinhold noted in *The New York Times* on Aug. 7 that even under the Carter plan, the poor "will continue to be separated into special medical and income maintenance programs outside the economic mainstream." This contrasts to the European democracies, he added, where "the 'welfare state' spreads a broad umbrella that covers rich and poor alike. While popular resentment over the cost of these programs is building, they do ensure that few people fall so low that they need to be uplifted by charity."[6]

Cost and Benefits of New Welfare Proposal

Cost is almost certain to be a major factor in congressional consideration of Carter's welfare proposal. In presenting the plan on Aug. 6, the President estimated that it would "have a total cost of $30.7-billion" or $2.8-billion more than the amount currently spent on the programs to be replaced. In addition, he said, $3.3-billion would be needed for an expanded earned income tax credit for low-wage earners in non-subsidized jobs.[7]

Sen. Russell B. Long (D La.), chairman of the Senate Finance Committee, disagrees strongly with the administration's cost estimates. In an address to businessmen in Washington on Sept. 15, Long said that Congress would be "foolhardy" to approve the proposal since its "actual cost" could well be "$60-billion or even $120-billion" over current expenditures. The following month the Joint Economic Committee released a study[8] concluding that the administration's estimate "is probably understated." The Congressional Budget Office on Nov. 29 predicted that the Carter proposal would cost almost $10-billion more than the programs it would replace.

It was charged that the critics often failed to take into account the added costs that would ensue if no welfare reform measure were enacted. Moreover, the Carter plan would have the advantage of bringing into the system thousands of Americans whose earnings are below the poverty level, currently

---

[6] Robert Reinhold, *The New York Times*, Aug. 7, 1977.

[7] Under existing law, the tax credit provides a rebate of 10 per cent to all who earn under $4,000, for a maximum credit of $400. The rebate is phased down by $1 for each $10 of earnings over $4,000 and disappears at $8,000. Carter proposed an additional 5 per cent credit on earnings between $4,000 and about $9,000 for a family of four. The credit would be available until income reached $15,600.

[8] "The Program for Better Jobs and Income—A Guide and Critique," Oct. 17, 1977, p. 24. The study was prepared for the Joint Economic Committee by University of Wisconsin professors Sheldon Danziger, Robert Haveman and Eugene Smolensky.

$5,995 for an urban family of four. Single individuals, childless couples, intact families and the working poor would be entitled to benefits. However, as a recent study for the Joint Economic Committee pointed out, welfare recipients in high-benefit states like New York, California and Massachusetts would "suffer a decline in benefits" unless the decline "is offset by state supplements." In only 12 southern states would there be an increase in benefits.

In 1976, state and local governments paid about $15-billion for welfare programs. Joseph A. Califano Jr., Secretary of Health, Education and Welfare, told the House Welfare Reform Subcommittee on Sept. 19 that "every state will be assured" of saving at least 10 per cent of its current welfare expenses in the first year of the program and 34 states could expect to save more. Many state and local officials recalled that Carter, as a presidential candidate, advocated complete federal funding of welfare and they complained that his proposal might actually increase their welfare costs.

While backers of the plan contend that its enactment would reduce fraud, overpayment and administrative costs, opponents typically argue that allegations of abuse and mismanagement in the existing system are unfounded or overstated. Through the use of computers and close scrutiny by federal, state and local officials, errors and abuses have been reduced significantly, they say. New York State's welfare and Medicaid expenditures, for example, were reported to have declined during the first six months of this year—for the first time in two decades.[10]

European Cradle-to-Grave Social Security

Many liberal critics consider the U.S. welfare system a failure on at least two counts: it is degrading to recipients and it has failed to eliminate poverty. They point out that social insurance programs—which include Social Security, Medicare, unemployment compensation and veterans' benefits—have been far more effective in reducing poverty. Social insurance programs, on which $141-billion was spent in fiscal 1976, brought the number of families in poverty down from 21.4 million to 12.5 million. Welfare benefits further reduced the number to 9 million families.[11]

---

[9] "Work, Welfare and the Program for Better Jobs and Income," Oct. 14, 1977, p. 17. The study was prepared for the committee by Professors Barry L. Friedman and Leonard J. Hausman of Brandeis University.

[10] The decline—from $2.56-billion in the first six months of 1976 to $2.4 billion in the first six months of 1977—is "believed to stem largely from a reduction in the public assistance caseload caused by tighter eligibility restrictions and stepped up efforts to control fraud and abuse," Richard J. Meislin reported in *The New York Times*, Dec. 2, 1977.

[11] Expenditures for social insurance and welfare exclude Medicare and Medicaid. For background on the incidence of poverty under both types of programs, see the Congressional Budget Office study "Welfare Reform: Issues, Objectives and Approaches," July 1977.

There have been proposals for many years that the United States discard its present income-maintenance systems and replace them with the kind of programs in effect in Europe. Sweden's social insurance system is often described as the most advanced in any democratic country. Parents receive about $1,100 at the birth of each child and further allowances during the first 16 years of the child's life. For the youngster who continues in school beyond 16, cash allowances and a combination of grants and study loans are available. Every Swede is protected through life by health insurance which provides free hospitalization, cash benefits during illness, medical services at minimal fees at polyclinics, and many medicines at production cost. In addition, unemployment insurance and industrial accident insurance, vocational retraining allowances and related benefits are available to all persons who work for wages or salaries. At 65, the worker may retire on a pension as high as 65 per cent of his or her highest earnings at work.[12]

These social insurance programs, initially intended to do away with any need for welfare or relief, have not succeeded in that regard. Relief programs have continued and grown in most of the European welfare states, although "except for England, they are relatively small," Robert Reinhold wrote. "While European countries generally spend about two or three times as much of their net national disposable income on social services as the United States, the proportion that they spend for relief is typically less than half of what it is here."

While explanations of why the United States has not adopted a similar all-encompassing income security system generally focus on the American commitment to *laissez-faire* economics and rugged individualism, cost factors must also be taken into account. In the United States, welfare and social insurance spending account for only about 15 per cent of the annual gross national product. In Scandinavian countries, it accounts for at least 40 per cent. To finance these services, Europeans are subject to income and sales taxes far higher than Americans pay. A Swedish worker earning about $12,000 a year, for example, pays over 70 per cent of his income in taxes.

Cost Concerns in Britain and Scandinavia

The economic security that the European welfare states provide has come about only through increasingly higher taxes. A recent survey by the Paris-based Organization for Economic Cooperation and Development shows that in Sweden today taxes equal 50.9 per cent of the gross national product, compared to 46 per cent in 1975 and 35.7 per cent in 1965. The comparable

---

[12] See Carl G. Uhr's "Economic Development in Denmark, Norway and Sweden" in Karl H. Cerny (ed.), *Scandinavia at the Polls* (1977), pp. 237-8.

U.S. figure is currently 29.6 per cent. Public spending for social programs has contributed to inflation, which is currently running at an annual rate of about 13 per cent in Sweden, 14 per cent in Britain and 10 per cent in Denmark. In the Netherlands, however, it is only about 6.3 per cent, about on par with the United States.

Many Americans see a disillusionment with welfare statism reflected in recent national elections in Scandinavian nations. In September 1976, Sweden's Social Democrats, the architects of the welfare state and the party in power since 1932, were narrowly defeated by a non-socialist coalition. A year later, Norwegian voters gave the dominant Labor Party only a one-seat majority in parliament. In Denmark, the Social Democratic Party, which leads a minority government, has been turning to the middle-of-the-road Liberals and Conservatives for support and away from the leftist Socialist People's Party.

The swing away from the political left in Scandinavia has not been accompanied by movement away from the welfare state, however. "Even the conservative parties in the Scandinavian countries no longer advocate a return to *laissez faire,*" an observer wrote. "...Neither do they urge any dismantling of the welfare state programs that their parliamentary representatives have participated, however grudgingly, in creating. Nowadays they concern themselves most of the time with such matters as reduction and reform of taxes, greater decentralization of the political decision-making process and of public administration and criticism of the large and growing government bureaucracy."[13]

Old and New World Attitude

EUROPEANS tend to view the U.S. system of welfare as a somewhat barbaric reminder of the 17th century British Poor Laws. The first of these laws, enacted in 1601, was based on the assumption that poverty was the result of sloth and that to "pamper" the indigent with assistance would discourage honest labor. All who could work, including children, were required to do so, those who refused were flogged. Whatever aid was dispensed to persons unable to work was given as charity and recipients were frequently looked upon with contempt.

From colonial days until the Depression 1930s, the Poor Laws, which held each locality responsible for its own needy, served as

---

[13] *Ibid.,* p. 220.

the basis for disbursement of public welfare in this country. To discourage itinerant begging, residency requirements for aid were established and the able-bodied were forced to work for their pittance. While improvements were made over the years, all pre-Depression assistance to the poor reflected the common view of indigent persons as shiftless or inferior to members of self-supporting families. It was a cardinal principle that public charity should provide only the minimum needed to sustain life; otherwise the pauper would be encouraged to remain a public charge. The only constant in the American attitude toward welfare before 1933 was "the belief that the poor were to blame for their condition."[14]

It was, ironically, the conservative German Chancellor Otto von Bismarck who introduced the first European program of social insurance for the needy. Legislation enacted in 1888 gave German workers protection against accidents, sickness and old age. While Bismarck's main objective in providing such income security was to destroy the liberal Social Democrats, his ideas provided a model for other European countries. Around the same time, France set up a program of children's allowances. Britain in the National Health Insurance Act of 1912 provided low-income workers with government-sponsored medical insurance. And Sweden, in 1913, sought to give the aged and disabled some protection through a pension system.

These measures gave Europeans nowhere near the economic security they now have, but they provided more protection than poor relief programs in the United States. Describing the American system, one observer wrote: "The welfare pattern throughout the nation on the eve of the Great Depression was a patchwork...of local, state and private activities.... The programs were scattered and the administration of them tended to be desultory...based on tax measures far from adequate to support them.... Poor relief generally was administered harshly and meagerly.... The poor had no clearly distinguishable right to relief of their distress, and the harshness of the laws themselves reflected a tendency to regard the poor as beyond hope of redemption."[15]

Federal Involvement Under the New Deal

Growing state, local and private aid to poor American widows, orphans, the aged, blind and disabled was totally overwhelmed by the Depression. The millions rendered destitute by unemployment of the family breadwinner and by loss of savings forced a new approach to public assistance. Upon assuming the presidency in 1933, Franklin D. Roosevelt and his

---

[14] Sar A. Levitan, Martin Rein and David Marwick, *Work and Welfare Go Together* (1972), p. 5.

[15] Wayne Vasey, *Government and Social Welfare* (1958), pp. 27-28.

New Deal "brain trust" gave major emphasis to job creation and social insurance rather than to outright relief for the needy. New Deal legislation underlines this preference.

The Federal Emergency Relief Act, the first national public assistance law, enacted shortly after Roosevelt took office in March 1933, provided some 18 million Americans with cash stipends averaging about $15 a week per family. The replacement of this act in 1935 with the Works Progress Administration (WPA), a job-creating agency, reflected Roosevelt's attitude toward welfare. In a letter to his close adviser, Col. E.M. House, in late 1934, Roosevelt expressed his concern about the Federal Emergency Relief Act. "What I am seeking is the abolition of relief altogether. I cannot say so out loud, yet I hope to be able to substitute work for relief."[16] The WPA and the Social Security Act of 1935 were both premised on the assumption that income benefits should be dependent upon work.

The Social Security Act, the federal government's first major involvement in income maintenance, set the pattern for what has remained the structural foundation of social welfare in the United States. The act provided insurance for the unemployed and the retired and public assistance for three categories of persons likely to be unable to earn a living for themselves: the aged, the blind and children in homes without breadwinners. Two distinct programs were embodied in the legislation. The first, consisting of unemployment and old age insurance, was contingent upon the individual's prior work and earnings. The second depended solely on need and was intended as a temporary program to be replaced eventually by social insurance.

The Depression also necessitated a series of programs to cushion the impact of unemployment and poverty in Europe. In Scandinavia, the 1930s witnessed a series of relief measures, including an easy-money policy, public works programs and subsidies to farmers. These programs can be seen as the beginning of the welfare states that came into being a decade later; they constituted a deliberate enlargement of the public sector to cope with economic displacement.

Nobel laureate Gunner Myrdal, the author of Sweden's comprehensive, postwar income-security system, compares the American view of welfare, as embodied in the Social Security Act, with the attitudes that developed in Europe. "Of crucial importance to the further development of income maintenance policies in the United States," he wrote, was Roosevelt's "unfortunate decision to follow the line of thinking of Bismarck...who had conceived this social program as...concerning only those

---

[16] Quoted by William E. Leuchtenburg in *Franklin D. Roosevelt and the New Deal* (1963), p. 124.

employed in the labor market and not endeavoring to cover the nation as a whole." In the European welfare states, he continued:

> The theory has been, at least since the 1930s, that well-planned social reforms are a profitable investment, for they improve the quality of life and thus the productivity of people and also preclude future public and private expenditures. Social reforms are therefore an investment.... This theory is almost missing in the United States.[17]

Rise of Welfare States in Postwar Europe

The creation of the welfare states in postwar Europe is often traced to a report submitted to the British government in 1942 by Sir William Beveridge. Entitled "Social Insurance and Allied Services," the report was based on the assumption that "the object of government in peace and in war is not the glory of rulers or of races, but the happiness of the common man." To ensure such happiness, Beveridge proposed a system of social insurance that would protect individuals and families from dependency and destitution. Public assistance might be necessary for a time to "meet all needs which are not covered by insurance" but welfare benefits "must be felt to be something less desirable than insurance benefits." Much of the Beveridge report, including National Health Insurance, was enacted after the Labor Party came to power in July 1945. The basic social welfare system remained intact during subsequent changes in government.

In addition to pension, unemployment and work-related disability benefits, European social security programs typically included children's allowances and comprehensive medical and dental care. The post-World War II European programs were based on two principles: "There must be a basic income floor for all those who have reached a certain age or who are otherwise entitled to assistance; and in addition there must be a benefit based on prior earnings. One tier prevents poverty; the second tier recognizes prior earnings or standard of living."[18]

But "even with the broad-based social insurance plans now in existence, 'welfare' has not been eliminated in Europe," Bette K. Fishbein of the Institute for Socioeconomic Studies has noted. "In Britain, the portion of the population on public assistance grew from 4.6 per cent in 1950 to 8.0 per cent in 1971. In Sweden, there was a decline from 8.4 per cent in 1940 to 4.1 per cent in 1949. The rate remained stable until 1965, when an

---

[17] Gunner Myrdal, "Welfare in America: The View From Sweden," *Saturday Review*, Dec. 11, 1976, pp. 46-47.
[18] Alvin L. Schorr, "Welfare Reform and Social Insurance," *Challenge*, November-December 1977, p. 19. Schorr is visiting professor at the National Catholic School of Social Welfare in Washington, D.C.

upward trend began, rising to 6.3 per cent in 1971."[19] As was the case in Europe, the growth of social insurance programs in the United States did not have the intended result of drastically reducing the number of persons needing public assistance. But the American system tended to make a greater distinction between welfare recipients and insurance beneficiaries than did its European counterparts.

In the United States, charges of fraud, waste, inefficiency and misuse of tax money have dogged public assistance programs since their inception. While both social insurance and welfare benefits have been greatly expanded over the years to give more aid to more people, it has been welfare that provoked the greatest controversy. The major complaint has been that too much money is being spent on too many undeserving recipients. Welfare costs rose from $316-million in 1937 to $3.3-billion in 1960 to almost $50-billion by 1976.[20]

Spending on major welfare programs by federal, state and local governments increased tenfold in the decade between 1967 and 1977 *(see p. 54)*. Despite the higher costs and the spate of new programs for the needy, the number of Americans designated as poor by the Bureau of the Census has remained at about 25 million. While it is argued that without these benefits millions more would have fallen below the poverty level, there has been growing concern that the programs have failed and will continue to fail in accomplishing their major goal of bringing the poor into the economic mainstream.

LBJ's Poverty War; Nixon's Family Plan

This same concern—that poverty for many was a trap which welfare and related programs could not remedy—was evident in President Johnson's "war on poverty." First announced in a message to Congress in January 1964 and implemented later that year in the Economic Opportunity Act, the law authorized separate programs to make a coordinated attack on the causes of poverty. It provided rehabilitative services, preschool education, training and jobs for young people and retraining for older, unemployed persons. In 1964 and 1965, the food stamp program, Medicaid and housing subsidies also became part of the administration's war on poverty.[21]

In many respects, the war on poverty and other Great Society programs constituted a recognition that the major premise behind the 1935 Social Security Act and its subsequent exten-

---

[19] "Social Welfare Abroad," a study by the Institute for Socioeconomic Studies, April 1975, pp. 14-15.

[20] For background, see "Future of Welfare," *E.R.R.*, 1975 Vol. II, pp. 856-857.

[21] For background, see Congressional Quarterly's *Congress and the Nation*, Vol. I (1965). pp. 1326-1329, and *Congress and the Nation*, Vol. II (1969), pp. 734-778.

Public Welfare Expenditures* 1967-1977

Program	1967 (in billions)	1977 (in billions)
Aid to Families with Dependent Children	$2.0	$10.3
Medicaid	$1.9	$17.2
Food Stamps	$0.1	$ 4.9
Housing	$0.5	$ 2.4
Supplementary Security Income for the Aged, Blind and Disabled	—	$ 6.9
Total	$4.5	$41.7

* By federal, state and local governments

Source: Figures submitted by Richard P. Nathan of the Brookings Institution in testimony to the House Welfare Reform Subcommittee, Oct. 12, 1977

sions—that social insurance would be the fundamental means of preventing poverty and that welfare would be a diminishing factor—had not been realized. Social insurance benefits tended to be based on how much individual contributors had paid into the system. As a result, those whose incomes had been higher would receive larger payments while the neediest, who had contributed little or nothing, would receive little or nothing in return. Thus during the 1960s the government stepped in with a host of "income-tested" programs, like food stamps, Medicaid and housing allowances which dispensed benefits solely on the basis of need.

By the end of the decade, the amalgam of programs designed to alleviate the plight of the poor was widely judged a failure. As Daniel Patrick Moynihan wrote: "The antipoverty program enacted in 1964 came to embody many of the ambiguities and uncertainties of an ambitious services strategy directed to the problems of poverty. A good deal of money was being expended. It could *not* be shown that it was going to the poor. It *was* going, to a large degree, to purchase services, which could *not* be shown to benefit the poor. And yet what was the alternative?"[22] The alternative, as conceived by Moynihan and presented to the nation by President Nixon on Aug. 8, 1969, was the Family Assistance Plan.

In outlining his proposal for an overhaul of the welfare system, Nixon called the existing system "a colossal failure. It breaks up homes. It often penalizes work. It robs recipients of dignity and it grows." Often referred to as "Nixon's good deed," FAP would have replaced Aid For Dependent Children with a

---

[22] Daniel Patrick Moynihan, *The Politics of a Guaranteed Income: The Nixon Administration and the Family Assistance Plan* (1973), p. 55.

cash grant of $1,600 annually for a family of four. Benefits were to be made available to "dependent families" headed by females or unemployed males and "working poor" families if annual earnings were below $3,920. Unemployed fathers and mothers of school-age children were required to accept job training or employment. Each state was required to make up the difference between a basic federal benefit of $1,600 and the state's existing benefit level. The cost of the program was estimated to be $8.2-billion in fiscal year 1970, an increase of $4.2-billion over the then-existing program.[23]

The Family Assistance Plan was approved by the House in 1970 and 1971 but died in the Senate where liberals wanted a much higher annual income guarantee and conservatives objected to any guarantee or demanded far stronger work requirements. In examining why FAP failed, Moynihan puts much of the blame on liberal Democrats and their supporters.

Since the plan's defeat, many of the reforms it was intended to promote have been realized. The food stamp program has been expanded to provide greater benefits to the working poor, work requirements for welfare recipients have been added, spending on job programs has increased substantially and in 1974, federally financed Supplemental Security Income benefits replaced a host of state programs assisting the needy aged, blind and disabled. Under prodding from the Department of Health, Education and Welfare, the percentage of ineligibles on the welfare rolls was cut from 10.2 per cent in 1973 to 5.5 per cent by the end of 1976. In the same period, cases of overpayment decreased from 22.8 per cent to 13.9 per cent and cases of underpayment from 8.1 per cent to 5.2 per cent.

Dilemmas in Reforming Welfare

P RESIDENT CARTER, like Nixon before him, made work the centerpiece of his welfare reform proposal. But the United States is still not willing to go as far as many Western European nations in providing jobs or income security for the unemployed. In Sweden, for example, there are extensive government-funded retraining programs to teach workers new skills. In addition to creating thousands of public-sector jobs, the Swedish government pays more than half of the wages of people under age 20 who are hired by private employers. In Holland, unemployment compensation amounts to 75 to 80 per cent of a worker's normal take-home pay for up to two years.

---

[23] See Gilbert Y. Steiner's *The State of Welfare* (1971).

Refusal to accept any job that is offered does not result in a curtailment of benefits.

Carter's Program for Better Jobs and Income combines work requirements with work incentives. Benefits for persons able but unwilling to work would be reduced while earned income tax credits would be offered to those in low-paying jobs. But a recent study prepared for the Joint Economic Committee questioned the efficacy of linking welfare and work requirements: "A work requirement and welfare reform really should not go together if one judges the cost effectiveness of the work requirement. Yet, if it is the political price necessary to achieve welfare reform, the benefits of the whole welfare reform package are likely to outweigh the costs of the work requirement."[24]

The impact of existing job requirement programs is disputed. The federal Work Incentive Program (WIN), begun 10 years ago and costing about $300-million a year, requires AFDC recipients over age 16 to register for training and placement. Last year, some 230,000 welfare recipients found jobs through WIN. About 20 states have enacted work requirement laws. One of the most stringent is in Utah where all able-bodied persons on welfare are required to work three days a week in public service jobs and two days looking for work in the private sector. Utah officials claim that between 1974, when the program began, and 1976, the welfare rolls have been reduced 16 per cent and the state has saved almost $350,000.

It is argued that work requirements and job incentives as a remedy for welfare dependency overlook two factors. The first, HEW Secretary Califano has pointed out, is that more than 90 per cent of current welfare recipients are unable to work because of old age, disability or the need to care for small children. The second factor is that there are not enough jobs. Carter's proposal to create 1.4 million public service jobs is viewed by liberal critics as inadequate and demeaning to those forced to take low-paying, "meaningless" jobs. The work requirement and the need for holders of public service jobs to look for non-subsidized employment has also aroused concern in organized labor that the availability of thousands of low-wage workers will cause employers to lay off highly paid union members.

On Nov. 14, President Carter endorsed the Humphrey-Hawkins "full employment" bill.[25] As originally introduced in 1974, the bill said every citizen had the right to a job and named the government the employer of last resort. It called for reducing

---

[24] "Work, Welfare and the Program for Better Jobs and Income," p. 114.
[25] Named for its chief sponsors, Sen. Hubert H. Humphrey (D Minn.) and Rep. Augustus F. Hawkins (D Calif.).

unemployment to 3 per cent within 18 months. Amid cries that such a measure would cost tens of billions of dollars a year and fuel inflation, the bill has undergone a series of changes. The revised legislation that Carter endorsed set as a goal an overall unemployment rate of 4 per cent by 1983 and committed the government to work toward it, without specifying how.[26]

Proposals to Guarantee a Minimum Income

To many advocates of welfare reform, proposals for a guaranteed minimum income are far more attractive and feasible than suggestions for a guaranteed job. The idea of a guaranteed minimum income, often referred to as a negative income tax, has been around for decades. It was included in Nixon's Family Assistance Plan and is in Carter's Program for Better Jobs and Income.

The idea is to provide persons below a specified income level with enough money to bring their income up to that level. In the United States, its leading advocate has been economist Milton Friedman, a political conservative. As outlined in his book *Capitalism and Freedom* (1962), everyone whose income falls below a certain level would receive a federal subsidy. To encourage recipients to work, they would be allowed to retain some part—perhaps half—of the income they earn in addition to the basic grant. When a "break even" point was reached—Friedman specified a figure of $3,000 for a family of four in 1962—all income would be subject to taxation. The program would be administered by the Internal Revenue Service, thus eliminating the need for the welfare bureaucracy.

A major question about the negative income tax is its impact on work incentives. Edgar K. Browning, an associate professor of economics at the University of Virginia, writes that the evidence "suggests that there would be a reduction in hours worked, but complete withdrawal from the labor force...would be unlikely on a significant scale."[27] An HEW study of 5,202 families in Seattle and Denver on the effect of a guaranteed income resulted in some surprises. Each family received a basic income of $3,800 to $5,600 a year; work incentives were included, and only part of the extra earned income was lost if the family breadwinner worked. The study, undertaken during the late 1960s and early 1970s, found that only about 6 to 7 per cent of the participants did not seek jobs when the tax rate on their earnings was 50 per cent.

The fact that a guaranteed annual income did not significant-

[26] For details on the Humphrey-Hawkins bill, see Congressional Quarterly's *Congress and the Nation,* Vol. IV (1977), pp. 708-709.
[27] Edgar K. Browning, *Redistribution and the Welfare System* (1975), p. 75. The study was published by the American Enterprise Institute for Public Policy Research.

ly reduce work incentives was perhaps less surprising than the
fact that the assurance of a basic income, which had been expected to keep families together, appeared to have the opposite
effect. Black, white and Mexican-American families participating in the experiment had substantially higher rates of
separation, divorce and desertion than others who were studied.

In his book on FAP, Daniel Patrick Moynihan contends that
the negative income tax is "an economist's idea," the method
preferred by most students of the "dismal science" for
redistributing income and solving the welfare problem. Public
opinion polls indicate that it was not particularly popular with
the majority of Americans. A Harris Survey in August 1967, for
example, found that 60 per cent of the people questioned said
they opposed a guaranteed income and only 28 per cent favored
it. Proposals for instituting a negative income tax have had
scant success in Europe, Bette K. Fishbein reported. "The
Netherlands rejected the idea in 1970 and no Scandinavian
country has given it serious thought." A principal reason, she
continued, "is the high level of social expenditures in these
countries.... Taxpayers are often more willing to pay for medical
services, housing and other specific programs rather than large
cash transfers. This is particularly true in countries with long-
established social welfare programs."

Debate Over Total or Only Partial Reform

Most Americans seem to agree that there is a need to reform
the present welfare system. But, Nick Kotz observes, "welfare
reform means very different things to different people. For some
conservatives and most of the public, reform means cutting
costs and reducing the welfare rolls. State and local welfare administrators want to unsnarl administrative red tape and shift
all costs to Washington. Academic reformers want to restructure
the present crazy quilt of programs into a rational system that
fulfills a whole list of idealized objectives.... More pragmatic
reformers want incremental improvements in the present
system rather than overall reform, which they think Congress is
unlikely to approve with any decent treatment for the poor.
Welfare recipients and their representatives...would welcome a
guaranteed minimum income and assured jobs paying a living
wage."[28]

As the Carter welfare reform proposal becomes subject to
more scrutiny, considerable attention is being given to the question of whether it would be preferable to completely overhaul
the present system (comprehensive approach) or to build upon
and improve existing programs (incremental approach). The

---

[28] "The Politics of Welfare Reform," *The New Republic*, May 14, 1977, p. 18. Kotz is co-
author, with Mary Lynn Kotz, of *A Passion for Equality* (1977).

administration's program is often described as comprehensive but actually calls for the consolidation of only three programs—AFDC, food stamps and SSI. The Joint Economic Committee concluded that "the Carter plan devotes insufficient attention to the coordination of the existing multi-purpose welfare system."

Most proposals for comprehensive reform would require the federal government to take over welfare costs now borne by state and local governments. New York Gov. Hugh L. Carey criticized the administration's proposal in testimony before the House Welfare Reform Subcommittee on Oct. 31 on the grounds that it would increase the number of persons on welfare and drive up costs in high-benefit states like New York. Estimates of the cost of "federalizing" welfare and establishing national standards range from $25-billion to $50-billion a year. This would mean that states where benefits are relatively low would have to pay more so that recipients in states like New York, California and Massachusetts could receive their accustomed benefits. As the uproar over New York's request for a federal bailout to prevent bankruptcy indicated, such an approach is likely to meet strong resistance.

The leading spokesman for an incremental approach to welfare reform is Richard P. Nathan, a senior fellow at the Brookings Institution who was Deputy Under Secretary of HEW in 1971-72. In testimony to the House Welfare Reform subcommittee on Oct. 12, Nathan contended that "the welfare mess has been overstated" and that it would be preferable to build upon the improvements that have been made in the past decade. Among other improvements, Nathan suggests expanding AFDC to cover all families headed by an unemployed male and providing minimum, national payment levels, making the food stamp program more flexible and including benefits for single persons and childless couples who are not covered by present programs.

Nathan and other incrementalists point out that a number of partial changes would be more feasible politically. According to the Congressional Budget Office report, "incremental reform is limited in scope and thus less threatening to existing interests." The administration's Program for Better Jobs and Income will doubtless face numerous demands for modification from these "existing interests." It is likely that in whatever final version emerges, there will be a strong commitment to the work ethic. As congressional scrutiny to date has indicated, equally close attention will be given to cost. Unlike the so-called European "welfare states," it appears that the United States is as yet unprepared to agree to a system mandating large-scale redistribution of income to help the poor and the disadvantaged.

Selected Bibliography

Books

Aaron, Henry, *Why Welfare Is So Hard to Reform,* Brookings Institution, 1973.

Campbell, Colin D. (ed.), *Income Redistribution,* American Enterprise Institute for Public Policy Research, 1977.

Cerny, Karl H. (ed.), *Scandinavia at the Polls,* American Enterprise Institute for Public Policy Research, 1977.

Friedman, Milton, *Capitalism and Freedom,* University of Chicago Press, 1962.

Jencks, Christopher, et al., *Inequality,* Basic Books, 1972.

LaPatra, J. W., *Public Welfare Systems,* Charles C. Thomas, 1975.

Robson, William A., *Welfare State and Welfare Society: Illusion and Reality,* Allen and Unwin, 1976.

Steiner, Gilbert Y., *The State of Welfare,* Brookings Institution, 1971.

Tyrell, E. Emmett Jr., *The Future That Doesn't Work: Social Democracy's Failures in Britain,* Doubleday, 1977.

Articles

Current History (issue devoted to Scandinavia and the Low Countries), April 1976.

Currie, Elliott, "A Piece of Complicated Gimmickry," *The Nation,* Sept. 17, 1977.

Etzioni, Amitai, "Toward a Swedenized America," *Saturday Review,* Dec. 12, 1976.

The Journal of the Institute for Socioeconomic Studies, selected issues.

Lekachman, Robert, "The Welfare Mess: Carter's Reforms Make Sense for Some, but the Cities Lose Again," *Politicks & Other Human Interests,* Nov. 22, 1977.

Lipman, Harvey, " 'Workfare' and Welfare," *The Nation,* Aug. 20, 1977.

Logue, John, "Welfare at the Crossroads," *The Progressive,* September 1977.

Rein, Martin and Lee Rainwater, "How Large Is the Welfare Class?" *Challenge,* September-October 1977.

Schorr, Alvin L., "Welfare Reform and Social Insurance," *Challenge,* November-December 1977.

Stewart, Walter, "The God That Failed," *Maclean's,* Jan. 24, 1977.

Reports and Studies

Comptroller General of the United States, "Food Stamp Receipts—Who's Watching the Money?" June 15, 1977.

Congressional Budget Office, "Poverty Status of Families Under Alternative Definitions of Income," June 1977.

——"Welfare Reform: Issues, Objectives and Approaches," July 1977.

Editorial Research Reports, "Future of Social Programs," 1973 Vol. I, p. 251; "Future of Welfare," 1975 Vol. II, p. 847.

General Accounting Office, "Ineffective Management of Welfare Cases Costing Millions," Dec. 28, 1976.

Joint Economic Committee of Congress, "The Program for Better Jobs and Income—A Guide and Critique," Oct. 17, 1977.

——"Work, Welfare and the Program for Better Jobs and Income," Oct. 14, 1977.

Mandatory Retirement

by

Nona Baldwin Brown

**Nov. 11
1977**

Editor's Note: The then-pending Supreme Court ruling discussed on pages 66 and 77, *McMann v. United Air Lines*, has since been issued. By a 7 to 2 vote, the court on Dec. 12, 1977, upheld the airline's retirement plan which requires employees to retire at age 60. The plan was put into effect before Congress in 1967 enacted the Age Discrimination in Employment Act.

The ruling presumably will affect other similar retirement plans that were established before the law was passed. However, the effect of the Supreme Court ruling may be nullified by Congress in its 1978 session when it takes final action on separate bills approved by the House and Senate to bar future forced retirement below age 70.

MANDATORY RETIREMENT

"TO LIVE is to work." The old aphorism, the credo by which Justice Oliver Wendell Holmes explained why he remained on the Supreme Court at age 90, the philosophic underpinning for the American work ethic, has suddenly become a political slogan for the nation's older citizens. With it, they have embarked on a fight to eliminate mandatory retirement for age from gainful employment as an immutable climax to productive years. In the process, they have raised far-reaching constitutional and economic questions: Is an extended working life a civil right? a personal necessity? or very possibly, an economic necessity for the nation? Politics and demographics may soon forge answers to these questions.

Congress, which normally recoils from sharp changes in existing programs, moved with unexpected speed this year to raise from 65 to 70 the age at which most workers can be compelled to retire. In less than five months from its final formulation in the House in June, both chambers overwhelmingly approved legislation to effect this change. The vote was 359 to 4 in the House and 87 to 6 in the Senate. The bills differed in some major respects but both versions agree in amending the Age Discrimination and Employment Act of 1967, which established legal protection against discriminatory employment practices for people of ages 40 through 64. The 1977 legislation (HR 5383) moves that upper age limit to 70.

Passage was preceded by several sets of hearings before both Senate and House committees—notably the House Select Committee on Aging, under the chairmanship of 77-year-old Claude Pepper (D Fla.)—dealing with the mandatory retirement issue. The House Education and Labor Committee, which initiated the legislation, drew heavily on evidence compiled by the Select Committee. In its report, the Education and Labor Committee said:

> Increasingly it is being recognized that mandatory retirement based solely upon age is arbitrary and that chronological age alone is a poor indicator of ability to perform a job. Mandatory retirement does not take into consideration actual differing abilities and capabilities....[1]

---

[1] Report on Age Discrimination in Employment Act of 1977, House Committee on Education and Labor, July 25, 1977, No. 95-527, Part I, p. 2.

However, HR 5383 did not totally abandon the compulsory age concept despite some strong philosophic support for the idea. On this matter, the report said:

> The committee has considered removing the upper age limit entirely but has decided that an increase to age 70 at this time is the best course of action. The age 70 limit is a compromise between some who favor removing the age limit entirely and others who are uncertain of the consequences of changing the present age 65 limit. Experience with the age 70 limit would give us more data and other facts to better evaluate the pro and con arguments on eliminating mandatory retirement entirely.

Opposition to the legislation did not surface until the Senate, which lacked Congressman Pepper's enthusiasm for the issue, began its consideration. Organized labor backed off from its original criticism *(opposite page)*, but the business community and the universities mounted intensive lobbying campaigns, based primarily on a dislike of sudden change in their retirement systems and fear that later retirement would block employment and promotion opportunities for younger people. The Senate version of HR 5383 therefore contained exceptions for highly paid executives and tenured university professors.

Whatever the final bill contains in detail—to be worked out in a House-Senate conference committee—it seems certain that President Carter will be handed a measure that will move the legal basis for mandatory retirement from age 65 to age 70. It also seems certain he will sign it, despite reported misgivings of some Cabinet advisers. Even in the Department of Labor, where support for the Pepper measure has been voiced publicly, there are many questions about its impact on chronic youth unemployment, sex discrimination and shifting consumer patterns.

Similar Moves by States and in Industry

Congress was not alone in what it did: this year three state legislatures—in Maine, New York and California—also debated measures modifying or eliminating retirement for age. The Maine lawmakers overwhelmingly approved a bill to remove the age factor for public employees, including school teachers, and then overrode Gov. James B. Longley's veto. The new law will go into effect July 1, 1978. New York legislation to eliminate age as a factor in both public and private retirement plans won approval in the Assembly but not the Senate.

California may provide the first large-scale test of the idea of eliminating age as a basis for compulsory retirement. The state legislature, after long and frequently acrimonious debate, voted to ban mandatory retirement at any age for both public and private employers, and Gov. Edmund G. (Jerry) Brown Jr.

Organized Labor's Neutrality

Organized labor ended up in a position of benign neutrality on the issue of forced retirement for age, after lining up initially with the U.S. Chamber of Commerce and other major business groups as the heavy hitters for the opposition. The AFL-CIO formally stated this opposition to both Senate and House committees because of fear that many labor-negotiated pension plans with mandatory age retirement provisions might be jeopardized by raising or eliminating the age limit. Labor wanted a special exemption, on the ground that these plans were voluntary agreements.

From the beginning, according to an analysis by A. H. Raskin of *The New York Times,* * many labor leaders were uncomfortable over this stance. The alliance with big business bothered them. The fact that AFL-CIO President George Meany is 83 was an embarrassing contradiction—which led Meany to an unaccustomed sidelines position. Some major unions, such as the steelworkers, were fundamentally opposed to mandatory age retirement and, Raskin said, "historically, organized labor has viewed with hostility any form of forced retirement."

When the House Committee on Education and Labor added a special proviso to the Pepper bill, allowing two years for union pension contracts to be revised to meet any new age standards, the AFL-CIO fell silent. The federation decided "to let nature take its course" instead of pursuing a losing political battle against the nation's elderly, Raskin reported. In addition, Lane Kirkland, the AFL-CIO Secretary-Treasurer and heir-apparent to Meany, let it be known that it was a mistake for labor to seek a special exemption.

*Sept. 21, 1977

signed the measure into law. Its provisions are already in effect for state workers; for the private sector, they become effective Jan. 1, 1978.

Twelve other states[2] have laws dealing with age discrimination in employment. For the most part these follow the pattern of the 1967 federal law that protects workers of ages 40 through 64. Cities that have taken similar action on behalf of their employees include Boston, Seattle, Los Angeles and Portland, Ore. "The public is for it," Seattle Mayor Wes Uhlman has said. "They see it as patently unfair to tell a person they can't work, especially with our Puritan ethic that says if you won't work, you're not worth anything."

In the private sector, the most striking event was an announcement in August by Connecticut General Insurance Corp.

---

[2] Alaska, Connecticut, Florida, Hawaii, Illinois, Iowa, Maryland, Montana, Nevada, New Jersey, New Mexico and South Carolina.

that most of its 11,900 employees no longer had to retire at 65. "Some of our employees want to continue their careers with the company beyond...normal retirement age," said the announcement, "and we recognize what a valuable resource they are." Connecticut General did make one exception: officers and field office managers are still required to retire at 65. "We did that," said company spokesman Donald Illig, "because we didn't want it to appear that there was any blocking of the [executive] pipeline."

The issue is also stirring in the courts. The Supreme Court will hear at least one case this term, *McMann v. United Air Lines,* on the right to work beyond a certain age. It involves the forced retirement of airline pilot Harris McMann of Fairfax, Va., at age 60 under the terms of United's pension plan. McMann is McMann is arguing that such action contravenes the Constitution's due process and equal protection clauses, and furthermore that it is illegal under the Age Discrimination in Employment Act of 1967.

Another case which may reach the court, *Bradley v. Vance,* involves mandatory retirement at age 60 for personnel of the U.S. Foreign Service. The U.S. Court of Appeals for the District of Columbia has ruled against the government, saying that since Civil Service personnel need not retire until age 70, the Foreign Service system "is patently arbitrary and irrational" and therefore unconstitutional. The appeals court did not object to mandatory retirement for age *per se.*[3]

Size of 'Gray Power' Lobby; Its Arguments

As the bills against "ageism" moved through Congress and state legislatures this year, opinion on both sides of the argument solidified and lobbying and political pressures mounted. The "gray power" lobby organized better and earlier than did the foes of the legislation. Spokesmen for elderly groups have testified frequently in recent years on the problems and needs of the elderly, speaking to Senate and House committees that were understandably sensitive to the 23 million potential voters who are now 65 or older.

The lobby has consisted of such disparate colleagues as actors John Wayne and Ruth Gordon, the Gray Panthers, the National Association of Retired Federal Employees, the National Council of Senior Citizens, the National Council on the Aging, the American Personnel & Guidance Association, and—the heavyweight among them, claiming a membership of 10 million—the American Association of Retired Persons/National Retired Teachers Association.

---

[3] *Bradley v. Vance,* U.S. District Court for the District of Columbia, Civil Action No. 76-0085, Memorandum dated June 28, 1977.

"Last month, I reached mandatory retirement age. I am still here. Anybody want to make something of it?"

Drawn by Joe Mirachi; 1977   The New Yorker Magazine, Inc.

These groups argued that mandatory age discrimination is costly to the nation and its old people. According to Professor James Schulz of Brandeis University, the national economy is deprived of at least $4.5-billion a year in lost income and purchasing power. Moreover, severe financial hardships are imposed on many retirees whose pension incomes are usually well below their earlier earnings. "Indeed," said the Senate report,[4] "for some, the opportunity to continue working has become a question of economic survival." It is further argued that there is no scientific reason for age 65 to have become the traditional retirement age *(see p. 69),* and that mere actuarial or administrative convenience is no reason for keeping it.

While making these practical and economic arguments for their position, supporters of the legislation generally leaned more heavily on ethics and human rights. Dr. Arthur Flemming, head of the U.S. Commission on Aging, said mandatory age retirement runs counter to the "Judeo-Christian ethic of dignity and worth of the individual." Claude Pepper stated the case this way: "Mandatory retirement is the cruel euphemism camouflaging age discrimination and forced unemployment.... It severs productive persons from the livelihood, shears their sense of self-worth and squanders their talents."[5]

"Mandatory retirement infringes on a basic right: the right to be judged on ability, not merely on age," Rep. Paul Findley (R Ill.), a cosponsor of the 1977 legislation, wrote in *The New York Times* on Sept. 14. This thought is echoed in arguments that forced retirement because of age is discriminatory and uncon-

---

[4] Report on HR 5383 of the Senate Committee on Human Resources, No. 95-493, issued Oct. 12, 1977.

[5] Speech to the National Council of Senior Citizens, Washington, D.C., June 6, 1977.

stitutional. Still another point made by backers of the legislation is that the loss of a job is a stress-producing event for the individual. The American Medical Association is cited in the Senate report as saying "there is ample clinical evidence that physical and emotional problems can be precipitated or exacerbated by denial of employment opportunities."

And finally, there is the political argument—no less powerful because it is implied rather than openly stated. The 23 million Americans 65 or older represent a big voting bloc. It is also known from election statistics that older people are more likely than others to cast a ballot on election day. The House Republican Research Committee said last July: "This is the type of people-oriented issue with which the GOP must be identified if it is to broaden its support base with the electorate." Democrats are equally interested. Indeed, public opinion seems to support the aims of the "gray lobby." A national poll of 1,603 persons conducted Oct. 26-27 by *The New York Times* and CBS News indicated that 52 per cent of the people want the law to forbid mandatory retirement below age 70 while 37 per cent do not, the newspaper reported Nov. 4.

Business, University Opposition to Change

Faced with a lost cause in the House, opponents of change mustered their arguments for the Senate. Businessmen and university spokesmen led the lobbying, citing primarily the economic and practical problems that might ensue from a five-year extension of the customary 65-year retirement age. Congress is moving too fast, they said. Such "drastic change" should not be enacted without further study. What business needs is less regulation, not more. George Skoglund, speaking for the Bank of America, said: "The underlying problem is that these laws constitute more and more regulation, more of government looking on and telling us how to manage."

Opponents said further that retirement at age 65 had become so deeply embedded in American society—through Social Security, many labor union contracts and private pension plans—that it would be too disruptive to change it. No one knew what costs or problems would follow. They also argued that:

> Extending the working years would slow down promotions and thereby thwart bright young people whose ideas and stimulation are necessary for growth.

> Without mandatory retirement at 65, corporations would be forced to make tough—and possibly humiliating—decisions on who is able to do his job, instead of letting the calendar solve the "deadwood" problem.

> It would be costly and difficult to manage pension funds and estimate employment costs, if there were no fixed date when employees would become entitled to benefits.

Having to make individual judgments about older workers would lead to a burst of age-discrimination lawsuits.

Keeping older employees would worsen the unemployment situation, specifically hurting young people, women and Affirmative Action programs. Spokesmen for both the National Association of Colored People and the Urban League joined the opposition on this basis.

Rebuttals to these arguments surfaced quickly and in various forums—speeches, press releases and political debate. They made these points:

If "ageism" is unfair and possibly unconstitutional, then discriminating against the elderly to benefit youth does not justify it.

The notion that older people could stay at work only at the expense of younger workers is false.

Mandatory retirement is just a crutch for the incompetent manager," asserted Mayor Wes Uhlman, "a tool used by the manager who doesn't want to do what any good manager should be able to do, that is: deal with an employee on a personal basis...."

The glut of Ph.D.'s is more responsible for scholarly unemployment than any possible impact of a change in the retirement age could be.

Population and Income Factors

T HE MODERN history of mandatory retirement and the use of age 65 as the magic number are both traced to Germany's famous Iron Chancellor, Otto von Bismarck. In the late 19th century, socialist turmoil beset many European governments and none was more hard-pressed than that of the conservative German chancellor. Hoping to stave off socialism, he instituted in 1889 the modern world's first comprehensive social insurance program, including both health insurance and an Old Age and Survivors Pension Act. Bismarck picked 65 as the year when old age began—cynics say because he knew that life expectancy then was only 45 years, so the government would not have to pay out much money.

Other European countries followed suit, most of them designating that same age. By the start of World War I, 10 European countries and several British dominions had adopted economic protection plans for the aged. Action lagged in the United States. While a few private pension plans were adopted, and New Jersey instituted a pension plan for teachers in 1896, it

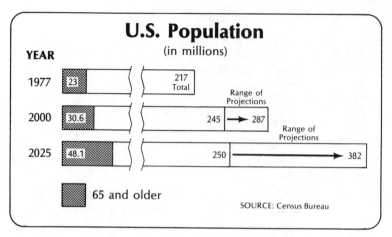

U.S. Population

(in millions)

YEAR

1977 · 23 · 217 Total · Range of Projections

2000 · 30.6 · 245 → 287 · Range of Projections

2025 · 48.1 · 250 ————→ 382

▨ 65 and older

SOURCE: Census Bureau

was not until after World War I that the movement toward pensioning elderly workers gained momentum. By 1931, 17 states and the territory of Alaska were providing old age insurance of some sort. But it was not until the Depression that major headway was made at the national level. Old age and unemployment insurance became major issues in the 1932 presidential campaign. After Franklin D. Roosevelt became President, he summoned experts to help develop the program which ultimately became the Social Security Act of 1935. Again, age 65 was used as the touchstone.[6]

Some say that age was selected quite casually, borrowed from the European precursors. Wilbur J. Cohen, then a congressional aide and later Secretary of Health, Education and Welfare (1968-69), wrote in his book *Retirement Policies Under Social Security* that there was very little consideration, pro or con, about the age when Social Security payments should begin. Robert J. Myers, one of the program's architects and for 20 years its chief actuary, recalls:

> "At the time, the Townsendites [followers of Dr. Francis E. Townsend, a California physician] were arguing that every American should collect a pension of $200 a month at 60, the money to be raised by a federal sales tax. But we knew that age was too low, because even with a smaller benefit than Dr. Townsend was advocating, the cost would have been enormous. At the time, too many people were working well beyond that age. We thought briefly about setting the age at 70, but decided that would be politically untenable, being so far above the age the Townsend Plan was agitating for. So we compromised on 65."[7]

Several big corporations—Eastman Kodak, General Electric, Standard Oil of New Jersey—had also picked 65 as the retire-

---

[6] While benefits were made available at 65, there was no provision in the act requiring retirement at that age. Congress amended the act in 1956 to permit women, and in 1961 to permit men, to retire at age 62 at 80 per cent of the monthly benefits that otherwise would be provided at 65.

[7] Quoted in *Dun's Review*, October 1977, p. 32.

ment year for pensions they had recently instituted. And so the pattern spread. Thus, after World War II, when retirement pension systems became a major goal of organized labor, the twin features of compulsion and age 65 became firmly implanted in major industries.

Unions were willing to accept forced retirement, usually at 65, for their workers in exchange for improved pension benefits—and lately, for the right to retire even earlier with full pensions. Corporations liked the personnel and bookkeeping tidiness of a flat rule for everybody: 65 and out. So even when pension-retirement plans are company-initiated, rather than the result of labor-management negotiations, the formula has been widely followed. According to Department of Labor estimates, some 21 million workers are now covered by private industry retirement plans, and 41 per cent, or 8.5 million, are affected by mandatory age retirement.

Continuing Growth of the Elderly Population

Much has changed in the working population since Bismarck's day. Not only is life expectancy longer in America today[8] but the entire age-mix of the population is tilting upward. Rep. Robert F. Drinan (D Mass.) has calculated that in terms of health and life expectancy, age 83 today is equivalent to what 65 was in Bismarck's time. The change is so striking that "graying of America" and the mobilization of "gray power" for "gray rights" are terms that have entered the political lexicon.

The specifics are these: of the nation's population in 1900, only 4.07 per cent (3.1 million people) was 65 or older; the percentage is now 10.8 and the number stands at 23 million. The Census Bureau projects an elderly population of 30.6 million in the year 2000 and 48.1 million in 2025, less than 50 years away. At that time the elderly may account for as much as 19.2 per cent of the total population, if one set of assumptions about national fertility proves to be correct.[9] If so, the nation's median age—now about 27—will rise by then to 41.8.

A population age-distribution chart shows a huge bulge in the age 20-34 category, a consequence of the postwar "baby boom" children now coming to maturity and into the job market. The baby boom reached its peak in the late 1950s and has been followed in recent years by a sharp drop in the birth rate and a consequent drop in the numbers of youngsters in the country.

---

[8] Life expectancy from birth is 68.7 for males and 76.5 from females; for those who reach 65, men can expect to live 13.2 years longer and women 17.5 years longer.

[9] The bureau makes a series of projections, each made on probable future fertility rates and other factors. See its publication *Projections of the Population of the United States 1975-2050*, Series P-25, No. 601, issued October 1975.

Teenagers and children made up nearly 40 per cent of the population in 1960 but may not account for 30 per cent in 2025.

The population profile half a century into the future is expected to show a huge bulge at the middle- and upper-age levels, the ages at which retirement from the job market becomes likely. A shrinking portion of the population will be working and feeding money into the giant pension systems. Within 50 years, one person will be drawing Social Security benefits for every two workers paying into the system. The ratio now is 3 to 1 and in 1950 it was 7 to 1.

Sources of Income for Older Americans

As Social Security legislation came into being, the principal problem with the elderly was poverty among people who had never earned very much or been able to save for the future. Even five years ago, one-fourth of the people over 65 had incomes below the official poverty level.[10] Today that figure has dropped to 15 per cent (it is 12 per cent for the general population); both Social Security benefits and private pensions have been fattened by inflation escalators. Studies indicate that the need today is not so much to avoid destitution as to maintain a decent living standard.

At the same time, the educational level of the elderly group has been rising. Where, a generation ago, many people over 65 were scarcely literate and only one out of five had a high school diploma, according to calculations made by *U.S. News & World Report*,[11] today one in three is a high school graduate and a great many have college degrees. Thus, observers note, the elderly today tend to be people accustomed to acting and doing, experienced in organizing, and self-confident enough to voice their concerns in the political forums.

It is difficult to get a precise picture of America's 23 million elderly citizens. It is equally difficult to find out much about the total "retired" population—which includes many people under 65. But a partial picture does emerge from available statistics and gerontological research. In the labor force today, 2.7 million workers are over 65 and one million of them are over 70. How many are holding or seeking part-time jobs is not known.

According to a recent White House survey,[12] 35 million Americans now get some sort of pension from either public or private sources, or both. The annual bill is now running around $133-billion, with the Social Security system paying $75-billion of that amount to retired workers or their survivors. As of June 1977, some 21.5 million of these recipients were over-65 retired

[10] Currently $2,964 for an individual.
[11] Issue of Oct. 3, 1977, p. 56.
[12] Cited in *Dun's Review*, October 1977, p. 83.

workers and their dependents.[13] The average Social Security benefit to retired workers that month was $240.17. While definitive figures are not available, it appears that more than half of all retirees do not have private pensions to supplement their Social Security income. There are also indications that, while retirees with two pensions may be receiving approximately half of their pre-retirement earnings, those on Social Security alone have only about a 40 per cent replacement of their generally lower earlier incomes.[14]

For many people, retirement is a much sought-after goal, a chance to get away from the daily work grind and to do all the pleasant things postponed through the working years. Most retirees, in fact, have retired as soon as they felt they could afford to, sometimes nudged by health problems. In a massive study of retirees conducted for the National Council on the Aging, 61 per cent said they chose to retire and 65 per cent said they had no desire to work any longer.[15]

There are differing opinions, however, on whether retirees are stimulated or traumatized by the end of regular work and earnings. "The key is psychological," remarked Paul Jackson, a consulting actuary in Washington. "It used to be when someone 55 retired, people looked at him a little funny if he hadn't had a heart attack or wasn't missing a leg.... Today, they look at him and say, 'Gee, he's got it made.' "[16]

The so-called trauma of retirement is "a myth without a shred of evidence to support it," asserts George Maddox, director of the Center for the Study of the Aging and Human Development at Duke University. Dr. Robert Atchley at the Scripps Foundation Gerontology Center at Miami University in Ohio, has observed: "In 12 years of research involving 5,000 people, I have not been able to document any serious psychological difficulties produced by retirement per se. ...A lot of people are anxious in anticipating retirement but most [of their fears] are not founded in fact."

On the other hand, Dr. Robert N. Butler, director of the National Institute on Aging, said: "For a significant number, retirement can be devastating. Many don't know what to do with themselves; they're jumpy and depressed. I call it the 'Willy Lohman' syndrome."[17] Statistics do show that the suicide

---

[13] Some 11.8 million recipients are under 65, including 1.8 million retired workers. Others are disabled workers or survivors and dependents. See *Social Security Bulletin*, October 1977, p. 1.

[14] Report of the House Select Committee on Aging, August 1977, Cmte. Publ. 95-91, pp. 25-29.

[15] "The Myth of Aging in America," 1975, study conducted by Louis Harris and Associates, Inc.

[16] Quoted by Jerry Flint in *The New York Times*, Oct. 2, 1977.

[17] Butler and Atchley are quoted by Lois Timnick in the *Los Angeles Times*, Sept. 10, 1977.

rate for white males age 65 to 69 is high: 36.5 per 100,000 population compared with a rate of 16 for all white males. But whether this phenomenon is related to post-retirement depression, to individual health problems, or to the cumulative effects of some chronic condition like alcoholism is not well documented yet. The American Medical Association says flatly that the "sudden cessation of productive work and earning power often leads to physical and emotional illness and premature death."[18]

In another aspect of the picture, considerable evidence has been amassed indicating that older workers are not necessarily the incompetent, deteriorating "deadwood" that personnel managers sometimes imply. Two studies referred to by the Senate Committee on Human Resources made this point. A New York survey of 33 state agencies in 1974 compared workers over and under age 65 with regard to absenteeism, punctuality, on-the-job accidents and overall job performance. It concluded that older workers were "about equal to and sometimes noticeably better than younger workers." The University of Illinois came to a similar conclusion in a study it had conducted earlier. "There was no specific age at which employees become unproductive and that satisfactory work performance may continue into the eighth decade," this study reported.

Duke researchers have found that older workers actually tend to be sick less frequently than others, although their illnesses are more likely to be serious and they are slower to recover. Senility affects only 15 per cent of all older people, usually as a corollary of some debilitating disease, it was further found. "The characteristics they seem to suffer most from," said Dr. Maddox, "is the tendency of society to treat them as though they are all alike."[19]

Experience of Firms With Older Workers

Forced retirement for age is not a universal practice. Companies that do not require it include Banker's Life and Casualty of Chicago, the Paddock Corp. of Arlington Heights, Ill., and even the huge steel industry where blue-collar workers have traditionally opposed mandatory age retirement. Their experience seems to bear out the picture of usefulness among those older people who want to keep on working.

The steel industry copes with the matter of competence and productivity of its workers by requiring annual physical examinations. "We don't have any problems with a worker staying on past 65 if he can pass the physical," a U.S. Steel Corp. official has said. "In fact, his productivity is probably greater." Not everyone shares this view. An oil company official

---

[18] Quoted in the Senate Committee on Human Resources' report *(see footnote 4)*, p. 4.
[19] Quoted by Ken Ringle in *The Washington Post*, Sept. 18, 1977.

remarked: "Let's face it. People's productivity begins to drop as they get older. You'd have a messy situation with no mandatory retirement forcing out the non-producers."[20]

Sen. S. I. Hayakawa (R Calif.), 71, and Ambassador Ellsworth Bunker, 83, who both support mandatory age retirement in principle, see it as a means of enabling older people to embark on second careers. Hayakawa, a former educator, revels in his new political life: "It is scary but extremely exhilarating. If you have ceased to be ready to face the frightening, then you become old." Ambassador Bunker, who recently completed negotiating a new Panama Canal treaty, has said: "I don't think there is any age limitation on a person's usefulness. It depends entirely on the individual."[21]

Forces Shaping Retirement Issues

F INANCIAL PROBLEMS of the Social Security system have provided an ominous background for the forced retirement issue. In the early 1970s, an accelerating trend toward early retirement and a recession-induced increase in the number of older people who lost their jobs combined to boost Social Security expenditures. The system is now paying $85-billion a year to retired and disabled persons, their survivors and dependents. Those benefits will rise to $180-billion by 1985, according to current projections.

Social Security payments exceeded income by $1.2-billion in 1975, by $3.2 billion in 1976 and, it is anticipated, $5.6-billion this year. The gap is currently made up by drawing on the Social Security Trust Fund reserves. But this fund, which stood at $40-billion in 1975, is expected to be exhausted by 1983. Clearly, the government will not let the Social Security system go bankrupt, so Congress this year has also been wrestling with various proposals for refinancing Social Security and insuring its stability well into the next century. Both the House and Senate have passed bills increasing Social Security taxes and benefits. Differences between the two bills are to be worked out in a House-Senate conference.[22]

The question has arisen, naturally, as to whether the Social Security system would benefit if the working years were extended and more people waited until later to start drawing benefits. The House Education and Labor Committee report

[20] Quoted in *Business Week*, Sept. 19, 1977, p. 39.
[21] Hayakawa and Bunker are quoted in *Time*, Oct. 10, 1977.
[22] It is likely that the conferees may not iron out their differences until early in the 1978 session of Congress.

said: "No estimate has been made of the possible effects of the [retirement age] legislation on Social Security outlays or receipts because of lack of recent and reliable information to make such an estimate...." However, the report went on to say that "some Social Security savings are likely to result...because some workers will forego private pensions and part or all of their social security benefits in order to continue working." The report of the Select Committee on Aging carries this point further, saying:

> With the ratio of workers to beneficiaries dropping significantly over the years, and the projected shortages in the trust funds, the economy and the country would seem better served if older workers who want to work and are able to work were permitted to do so.

Secretary of Commerce Juanita M. Kreps has wondered whether it might not be advisable, in view of both actuarial and population trends, to consider moving the age of entitlement to full Social Security benefits gradually from 65 to 68. This, she said, would "enormously reduce the Social Security burden." The outcry against such a "breach of faith" with present and future retirees was loud and immediate, although there is evidence that her suggestion is gaining some acceptance. In September, there was a Republican effort to revive the Kreps proposal, and some favorable editorial comment has appeared.

Growing Trend Toward Early Retirement

Since the early 1960s, the trend toward early retirement—well before age 65, and today even before age 60—has picked up momentum. In 1956 only 2.2 per cent of all Social Security benefits were paid to people under age 65. By 1972, the figure was above 50 per cent. Of the new awards made in 1974, some 72 per cent were for reduced benefits under age 65.

The trend has been furthered by a growing number of large union-negotiated pension plans that encourage early retirement by offering full pensions after a given length of time—often 30 years of work by age 55. The auto and steel workers have been leaders in the "30 years and out" drive. At General Motors, Congress was told, the average retirement age for wage earners was 67 in 1954 and for salaried workers it was 63. Today, they both retire at 58 or 59. Only 11 per cent of the salaried workers at General Motors stay on the job long enough to reach mandatory retirement age, and a mere 2 per cent of the blue-collar workers do. At Ford, more than 89 per cent of all employees retire before age 65, and only 2 per cent stay to the mandatory retirement age of 68. The federal government, with its 70-year age limit for most employees, reported that in 1976 the average age for all retirees was 58.2 years.

It appeared to the House Select Committee on Aging that most people opting for early retirement are those receiving both private pension and Social Security benefits. They retire as soon as they can afford to so they can "go for the good life." A Social Security survey in 1968 did show that more than half of the early retirees questioned said that health was the reason for quitting work early, but there is no data correlating this finding with pension levels. The House Select Committee, in reporting the survey, concluded nonetheless that "the primary reason for the trend toward early retirement would seem to be eligibility for a pension connected with a desire for leisure time to pursue other interests."

Why, then, the push for eliminating mandatory age requirements, when so few workers wait to be pushed out? John Martin, former head of the U.S. Commission on Aging, responds: "We don't want this legislation passed because we want all people over 65 to work. We just want to have the choice of working, like anyone else."

Legal-Right Questions Before the Courts

The immediate question of raising the mandatory retirement age to 70 is almost settled. But long-range questions remain and will undoubtedly surface in many ways. There is, first, the question of the constitutionality of age discrimination. Court cases decided so far have not upheld the thesis that "ageism is like sexism or racism," or, as some describe it, the last great constitutional barrier to full civil rights by all citizens. The Supreme Court, in upholding a Massachusetts law permitting the forced retirement of a state police officer at age 50, said in 1976 that the elderly "have not experienced a 'history of purposeful unequal treatment' or been subjected to unique disabilities on the basis of stereotyped characteristics not truly indicative of their abilities." The elderly, in other words, are not a "suspect classification" like blacks or women.[23]

The McMann case now before the Supreme Court (see p. 66) will not necessarily rest on the constitutional issue, but it is important for other reasons. Although the pleading mentions discrimination under the due process and equal protection clauses of the Constitution, the plaintiff's principal argument focuses on the Age Discrimination and Employment Act of 1967, in which a provision on pension plans is in dispute. United Air Lines, the defendant, interpreted the provision to exempt pension plans already in effect which required retirement at 65. If the Supreme Court were to uphold United's position, pension plans now in existence might conceivably be exempt from current legislation changing the mandatory retirement age.

---

[23] *Massachusetts v. Murgia,* 427 U.S. 307 (1976).

Federal Retirement Rules

Most employees of the federal government are required to retire at age 70, but there are many exceptions. While 70 applies to Civil Service personnel, 60 is the retirement age in the Foreign Service. And for FBI agents it is 55.

Congress imposes no age limit on membership. Twenty-one of the 100 senators and 38 of the 435 representatives are 65 or older.* At 81, Sen. John L. McClellan (D Ark.) is the oldest member of Congress, followed by Sen. Milton R. Young (R N.D.), who turns 80 on Dec. 6. Five of the nine members of the Supreme Court are over 65: Chief Justice Warren E. Burger (70) and Associate Justices William J. Brennan (71), Thurgood Marshall (69), Harry A. Blackmun (69) and Lewis F. Powell Jr. (69).

Likewise, no upper age limit is imposed on the President. Only two Presidents took office when they were 65 or older—Buchanan (65) and William Henry Harrison (68)—but several remained in office after reaching 65. Eisenhower served till age 70 and became the oldest man to hold the office.

*Two others become 65 before the end of the year—House Speaker Thomas P. (Tip) O'Neill Jr. (D Mass.) and Rep. Clement J. Zablocki (D Wis.).

In contrast to the Supreme Court's ruling in the Massachusetts case last year, the House Select Committee concluded in its report that age "should be as protected a classification as race and sex." The argument "that everyone ages and no particular group is singled out for discrimination ignores the fact that discrimination solely on the basis of age is wrong," the committee reasoned. "If mandatory retirement because of age...is not to be declared unconstitutional by the courts, then Congress should act to make such practice illegal."

The current legislation directs the Secretary of Labor to undertake a study of the economic effects of total elimination of age criteria for retirement, and to report back to the Congress within two years. One question to be answered is: How big an impact on the labor market will result from raising, or voiding, the mandatory retirement age limit? The Department of Labor estimates that perhaps 200,000 workers might be added each year to the labor force, which currently stands at 98 million. Other estimates have been as low as 125,000. A Sears Roebuck employee poll indicated that one-third or more of the elderly would like to work if they could obtain jobs—a finding that suggests to some the number could be as high as 2.8 million. The critical question is whether these added workers would be absorbed into the job market or whether they would cause a commensurate jump in unemployment.

How can pension plans, both public and private, find adequate funds in the future if the trend continues toward earlier retirement and higher benefits? General Motors, for example, has found a situation similar to that facing Social Security: in 1967 the ratio of GM workers to pensioners was 10 to 1, but by the early 1990s it is expected to be only 2 to 1.

Can management cope with the uncertainties that may result from increasing or eliminating mandatory age retirement? In objecting to current legislation, many corporate representatives cited experience rather than statistics. The general feeling in Congress seemed to be that both the human and financial aspects of the situation were quite manageable. Only time would tell whether pension costs would rise or fall, or whether payrolls would be affected by having proportionately more highly paid older workers.

Demographic Imperative: An Aging Nation

"It's a scary thing," Allen Selmin, 71, a member of the Tennessee Commission on aging, has said. "With people living longer and no work force coming on, you're going to have fewer people working and more and more old folks. It can't keep up. The answer is you can't retire them. You'll have to have them work until they die or until they're too sick."[24] Selmin was speaking of a future that is only 40 or 50 years away, as the demographic charts indicate.

Peter Drucker, social scientist and prominent writer on the problems of the elderly, wrote recently that "except perhaps in the event of a truly catastrophic depression, labor supply for the traditional blue-collar jobs will increasingly be inadequate even if present blue-collar workers are willing to stay on the job beyond age 65.... We will have to consider what incentives we need to encourage people...to postpone retirement...."[25] The concern is focused on what will happen when today's young people of the baby boom reach their sixties. If they all retire—early or even at 65—the number of supporting workers will be too low and the tax level required for pension support too high to be politically tolerable.

What lies ahead, then, may well be something more than today's gray rights' advocates have had in mind. The January 1977 *Morgan Guaranty Survey* said: "Working life in this country in the future may well grow longer rather than shorter, as many Americans have blithely assumed. About the time today's 35-year-olds reach the age when their parents retired, an added stretch of years on the job may be required." This, observers noted, would simply mean a return to the work force characteristics of the first decade of this century, when two-thirds of all American workers over age 65 stayed at their jobs.

---

[24] Quoted by Katherine Barrett in Memphis *Commercial-Appeal*, July 4, 1977.
[25] Peter Drucker, writing in *The Wall Street Journal*, Sept. 15, 1977.

Selected Bibliography

Books

Atchley, R. C., *Sociology of Retirement,* John Wiley & Sons, 1976.
Butler, Robert N., M.D., *"Why Survive? Being Old In America,"* Harper & Row, 1976.
Cohen, Wilbur J., *Retirement Policies Under Social Security,* University of California Press, 1957.
Drucker, Peter, *The Unseen Revolution,* Harper & Row, 1975.

Articles

Colamosca, Anne, " 'Gray Rights' Retirement Fight," *Dun's Review,* October 1977.
Congressional Quarterly Weekly Report, Sept. 3, 1977, pp. 1874-1878.
Eglit, Howard, et al., "Is Compulsory Retirement Constitutional?" *The Civil Liberties Review,* fall 1974.
Flint, Jerry, series of articles in *The New York Times,* July 10, Aug. 11, Sept. 24, Oct. 2, 1977.
Ladd, Everett Carl Jr. and Seymour Martin Lipset, "Many professors would postpone retirement if law were changed," *The Chronicle of Higher Education,* Nov. 7, 1977.
Maddox, George L. and Gerda G. Fillenbaum, "Work after Retirement," *The Gerontologist,* Vol. 14, No. 5, October 1974.
Maddox, George L. and Linda K. George, "Subjective Adaptation to Loss of Work Role: a Longitudinal Study," *Journal of Gerontology,* 1977, Vol. 32, No. 4.
McCraw, M. Louise, "Budgets for Retired Couples Rose Moderately in 1976," *Monthly Labor Review,* October 1977.
"Now, the Revolt of the Old," *Time,* Oct. 10, 1977.
Shapiro, Harvey D., "Do Not Go Gently...." *The New York Times Magazine,* Feb. 6, 1977.
"The Ax for Forced Retirement," *Business Week,* Sept. 19, 1977.
U.S. News & World Report, "Big Fight over Retirement," Oct. 3, 1977; "New Retirement Rules: Their Impact on Business, Workers," Nov. 7, 1977.

Reports and Studies

Editorial Research Reports, "Plight of the Aged," 1971 Vol. II, p. 865; "Retirement Security," 1974 Vol. II, p. 967; "Pension Problems," 1976 Vol. I, p. 363.
House Committee on Education and Labor, report accompanying H.R. 5383, "Age Discrimination in Employment Act Amendments of 1977," Rept. 95-527, Part I, July 25, 1977.
House Select Committee on Aging, "Mandatory Retirement: The Social and Human Cost of Enforced Idleness," August 1977, Comm. Publ. No. 95-91.
Senate Committee on Human Resources, report accompanying H.R. 5383, "Amending the Age Discrimination in Employment Act of 1977," Rept. No. 95-493, Oct. 12, 1977.
Social Security Administration, "Beneficiaries Affected by Annual Earnings Test in 1973," Vol. 40, No. 9, September 1977.
United Nations General Assembly "Question of the Elderly and the Aged," Report of the Secretary General, Nov. 8, 1973.
William Mercer Inc., "Employer Attitudes Toward Mandatory Retirement," June 1977.

Youth UNEMPLOYMENT

by

Sandra Stencel

Oct. 14
1977

YOUTH UNEMPLOYMENT

T HIS MONTH the Department of Labor will begin recruiting unemployed youths for a wide variety of jobs in public parks, forests and recreation areas. By the end of the year nearly 8,000 young people are expected to be enrolled in the program. Thousands of other jobless youths will be put to work in community improvement projects ranging from rehabilitation of public buildings to insulation and repair of low-cost housing. These young people will be the first hired under a $1-billion youth employment and training program approved by Congress last summer. By next September 200,000 young people are expected to be working in jobs or enrolled in training programs authorized by the Youth Employment and Demonstration Projects Act of 1977. An additional 250,000 teenagers and young adults could be enrolled if Congress appropriates an additional $500-million which President Carter has requested for the program.

Community leaders, government officials and social scientists generally applauded the new program, but many caution that it will not be a cure-all for persistent high rates of joblessness among the nation's 23 million young workers (ages 16 to 24). The Bureau of Labor Statistics reports that more than three million of them are unemployed. This age group makes up only a quarter of the nation's labor force but accounts for nearly half of the unemployed. The overall unemployment rate in the United States during September was 6.9 per cent, but far higher among the nation's teenagers (18.1 per cent) and especially among black teenagers (37.4 per cent).

Some say such statistics understate the scope of the problem. For one thing the figures do not include the scores of youngsters who become discouraged and quit looking for work. Also excluded are those who want full-time jobs but find only part-time work, and the tens of thousands of college graduates who must take jobs outside their chosen fields *(see p. 96)*.

Consequences and Causes of Unemployment

The consequences of high rates of unemployment among youth were spelled out by President Carter upon signing the 1977 Youth Employment Bill at a ceremony in the White House Rose Garden on Aug. 5. "If a young person...cannot get a job in the formative years of life," Carter said, "there is a feeling of despair, discouragement, a loss of self-esteem, an alienation from the structure of society, a lashing out against the authorities who are responsible...." Sometimes this "lashing out" takes a violent form. More than half of all serious crimes[1] in the United States are committed by youths under the age of 18. Though offenders come from every ethnic group and environment, the majority are non-white kids from urban slums. Until America solves the problem of youth unemployment, said Sen. Hubert H. Humphrey (D Minn.), "there is absolutely no way" to stop crime.[2]

Today's job situation can be attributed partly to the high birth rates in the 1950s and early 1960s. According to the Census Bureau, there are now four million more Americans of ages 16-24 than when this decade began. But there are other factors, as noted in a recent study by economist Anne McDougall Young. She reported that while the number of youths increased by one-third between 1966 and 1976, their representation in the work force rose by one-half.[3] The winding down of the war in Vietnam and the elimination of the draft put more young men in the civilian job market. From 1969 to 1975, according to Donald Eberly, a senior policy analyst for the government agency Action, the number of 18-to-24-year-olds in the armed forces dropped by 1.26 million.[4] Not only were fewer young men in uniform but apparently many left school to seek work when the draft ended.

Many of these youths hit the job market at the very time the United States was hit by recession in 1974-75. In addition, there was increased competition from the growing number of women entering or reentering the labor force.[5] Even during times of greater prosperity youth unemployment has been much greater than the national average. Between 1965 and 1973, viewed as economic "boom" years, youth unemployment remained at about 15 per cent, while the national unemployment rate fluctuated between 3 and 5 per cent.

Federal Work Programs for Young People

The federal government already spends billions of dollars each year on job and training programs for unemployed youths. During fiscal year 1976 some two million young people took part in programs under the Comprehensive Employment and Train-

---

[1] Murder, rape, aggravated assault, robbery, burglary, larceny, motor vehicle theft.
[2] Quoted in *The Christian Science Monitor*, March 7, 1977. See also "Crime Reduction: Reality or Illusion," *E.R.R.*, 1977 Vol. II, pp. 537-556.
[3] Anne McDougall Young, "Students, Graduates and Dropouts in the Labor Market, October 1976," *Monthly Labor Review* (Department of Labor publication), July 1977, p. 40.
[4] Donald Eberly, "National Service: Alternative Strategies," *Armed Forces and Society*, May 1977, p. 448. Action is the federal agency that directs a number of volunteer programs, including the Peace Corps.
[5] See "Women in the Work Force," *E.R.R.*, 1977 Vol. I, pp. 121-142.

Youth Unemployment Rates

	All Youths 16-19	Black and Minority Youths 16-19	All Youths 20-24
1950	12.2%	—	7.7%
1955	11.0	15.6%	7.0
1960	14.7	24.3	8.7
1965	14.8	26.5	6.7
1970	15.2	29.1	8.2
1972	16.2	33.5	9.3
1974	16.0	32.9	9.0
1975	19.9	36.8	13.6
1976	19.0	37.1	12.0
1977 (Sept.)	18.1	37.4	10.7

Source: Bureau of Labor Statistics

ing Act of 1973 (CETA). These included 160,000 in public service jobs, 500,000 in work experience programs, 200,000 in on-the-job and classroom training programs, 40,000 in the Job Corps *(see p. 94),* and 1,135,000 in the Summer Neighborhood Youth Corps programs.[6] Responding to an administration request, Congress on May 5 added $68-million to the fiscal 1978 Job Corps budget,[7] thereby increasing the number of trainees to 30,000 from 22,700.

In July Congress passed the 1977 Youth Employment Act, incorporating many of the features of a youth employment package that President Carter had proposed in March to complement his economic stimulus plan.[8] The bill added new provisions—Title VIII—to the Comprehensive Employment and Training Act to authorize a year-round program of conservation-related work modeled after the Depression-era Civilian Conservation Corps *(see p. 91).* A total of 22,000 unemployed youths, 16-23, are expected to be enrolled in the Young Adult Conservation Corps by September 1978. The

[6] Congress in June 1977 enacted a law providing for a simple extension through fiscal 1978 for existing programs under the Comprehensive Employment and Training Act.
[7] Included in a $20-billion supplemental fiscal 1977 appropriations bill containing funding for job programs and other elements of President Carter's economic stimulus plan.
[8] See *Congressional Quarterly Weekly Report,* May 28, 1977, pp. 1072-1073, and July 30, 1977, pp. 1595-1596.

enrollees will be paid the minimum wage for work on a variety of conservation projects. Most corps members will continue to live at home during the first year of operation; only about a quarter of the enrollees will be housed at residential projects. The Department of Labor, which administers the corps, hopes to open more residential camps in 1980 and 1981.

Some critics of the young Adult Conservation Corps believe that the long-range benefits to the participants might be negligible, since the skills that will be learned might not be transferable to jobs in urban areas. They further say that urban youths may benefit more from two experimental one-year projects created under Title III of CETA: the Youth Community Conservation and Improvement Projects and the Youth Employment and Training Programs. Both give preference to the economically disadvantaged, especially minority youths who have a hard time finding jobs. Both stress the role of neighborhood and community-based organizations and encourage the involvement of local labor organizations.

It is estimated that the Youth Community Conservation and Improvement Projects will employ 17,000 youths aged 16-19 in supervised projects of obvious benefit to the local community, such as rehabilitation of low-income housing. Some 112,000 low-income youths aged 16-21 are expected to benefit from a variety of projects authorized by the Youth Employment and Training Programs. In addition to work experience, participants will be provided with job counseling, on-the-job training and placement services.

The Youth Employment and Training Programs are intended to help youths overcome some of the most obvious obstacles to their employment—lack of marketable skills, lack of job experience, poor work habits, problems coordinating school and work. Another barrier to employment is the high dropout rate among disadvantaged and minority youths. The 1977 Youth Employment Act sets aside $115-million to test the feasibility of guaranteeing low-income students, 16-19, year-round jobs as an incentive to finish high school. The experimental, 18-month program—known as Youth Incentive Entitlement Pilot Projects—will begin in January 1978 and provide jobs for about 20,-000 students and dropouts who are willing to return to school. The jobs will pay the minimum wage and will average 20 hours a week during the school year and 40 hours a week during the summer.

Special Difficulties Facing Black Youngsters

About 60 per cent of the participants in the new youth employment programs will be blacks and other minorities, according to Secretary of Labor F. Ray Marshall. Unemployment

Youth Unemployment in Europe

Youth unemployment is also a serious problem in Europe. When the leaders of Britain, France, West Germany, Italy, Canada, Japan and the United States met at an economic summit conference in London last May, youth unemployment emerged as one of the principal topics of discussion. The seven leaders pledged to exchange ideas on providing the young with job opportunities.

Currently more than one-third of all unemployed persons in Europe are under 25 years of age. In Britain more than half a million young people are out of work, equal to 35 per cent of all the unemployed. French youths account for more than one-third of the jobless in that country. French President Valery Giscard d'Estaing said finding jobs for young people was the "No. 1 national priority."

Joblessness among the young in Italy is considered a threat to the political and social order. It is estimated that of the 132,000 Italians who will graduate from college next year, only 75,000 will be able to find jobs. As a result, Italian universities have become hotbeds of violence and extremism.

among non-white youths is the highest of any single component in the U.S. labor force. On Sept. 7, President Carter told the black members of Congress—the Congressional Black Caucus—that he regarded the plight of jobless black teenagers his "most important domestic issue right now." Carter was responding to recent criticism from black leaders that his administration has ignored the problems of blacks and other poor people. Adding to Carter's difficulties with the black community was the release Aug. 31 of a Department of Labor survey of summertime employment trends among youth.

The overall unemployment situation among youths aged 16-21 had improved slightly—falling to 15.3 per cent in July 1977 from 15.9 per cent in July 1976, the survey showed. But the improvement took place almost entirely among white youths, whose jobless rate fell to 12.6 per cent from 13.8 per cent a year earlier. Among blacks, however, there were 100,000 more jobless youths this past summer than the previous summer. The unemployment rate among black youths reached 34.8 per cent, the highest for any July on record.

The situation was even worse in some of the nation's largest cities. In New York 86 per cent of the non-white teenagers did not have jobs in July. Herbert Bienstock, a regional commissioner of the Bureau of Labor Statistics, characterized New York as "the non-working teenage capital in the country."[9] The high rate of joblessness among teenagers was said to have con-

---

[9] Quoted by Sen. Jacob Javits (R N.Y.) in a press release issued Aug. 4, 1977.

tributed to the outbreak of looting during the city's power blackout in July.

Despite the billions of dollars already spent on work programs aimed at minority youth, young blacks are relatively worse off now than they were 20 years ago. Herbert Hill, formerly the national labor director of the National Association for the Advancement of Colored People (NAACP) and now a professor at the University of Wisconsin, has said that if the situation does not improve soon "a large part of a generation of urban black youths will never enter the work force." Dr. Robert S. Browne, director of the Black Economic Research Center, pointed out that many of these youths come from families that have been without jobs for three generations or more. "What's developing is an entrenched social and economic underclass...," he said. "It's going to be awfully hard to get at."[10]

Persons trying to account for high rates of joblessness among black youths point to the effects of the ghetto environment, continuing racial discrimination and the lack of stable, job-oriented family patterns. Many black leaders blame inner-city schools, which, they say, produce graduates who are scarcely able to read or write. In recent years several factors have intensified the employment problems of black youths. These include (1) the flow of jobs from central cities to neighboring suburbs, and from the North and upper Midwest to the South and Southwest; (2) fewer low-paying, low-skill jobs; and (3) the effects of the recession. Industries in which blacks traditionally have been employed in large numbers, such as steel and textiles, were among the hardest hit by the recession.

Compounding the problem has been the high black birth rate, which is about triple that for whites. Arnold Packer, an Assistant Secretary of Labor, noted Sept. 7 in a report to President Carter on black unemployment that the black teenage population had increased by 43 per cent during the past 10 years. For white teenagers the increase was only 17.6 per cent.

Deprived of jobs, many young blacks become alienated from society and develop hostile attitudes toward it. Many spend their days "hanging out" on the streets, where they often turn to crime. The high unemployment rate among ghetto youth is generally blamed for the new rash of gang activity in the nation's cities. According to a study in 1976 by Walter B. Miller of the Harvard Center for Criminal Justice, "violence perpetuated by members of youth gangs in major cities is at present more lethal than at any time in history."[11] Some observers

---

[10] Hill and Browne were quoted in *The New York Times;* Hill on Sept. 11 and Browne on Sept. 21, 1977.

[11] "Violence by Youth Gangs and Youth Groups in Major American Cities," summary report, April 1976, p. 8. See also "Violence in the Schools," *E.R.R.*, 1977 Vol. II, pp. 581-600.

say that resentment among black youths has been intensified by the knowledge that growing numbers of blacks are escaping the poverty of the ghetto and moving into the middle class. "The awareness that many blacks have been successful," explained Harvard sociologist David Riesman, "means that the underclass is more resentful and more defiant because its alibi isn't there."[12]

Disdain for Work Ethic Among Teenagers

In a controversial article in the September 1977 issue of *Commentary*, Midge Decter declared that even if there were jobs for everybody, sizable numbers of black youths still would not be working.

> For large numbers of those young men on street corners [Decter wrote] it does not pay to take a job. Not only because there is nothing much they are qualified to do; and not only because welfare payments are at least adequate to keep them housed and fed; and not only because they have increasingly been brought up in, and seem content to perpetuate, a system of being kept by women; but because so many of them have access, or the occasional promise of access to a different kind of money—money sometimes dangerously, but always easily, come by.[13]

These youngsters, like those described in Claude Brown's book about his growing up in Harlem, *Manchild in the Promised Land* (1965), would not be caught dead holding down a regular job. They prefer to scratch out a living on the streets as con-artists, muggers, thieves, drug pushers, pimps and prostitutes. "This list of employments is not very pretty..." Decter wrote, "but one pays those young men less than proper respect to imagine that President Carter can so easily afford the means to buy them away from their present life."

Many people would dispute Decter's arguments,[14] but others contend that the disdain for work is pandemic among teenagers—white and black. School guidance counselors report that teenagers are more demanding about the hours they work, the money they earn and the kind of work they do. Alan Ribnick, vocational counselor at Yates High School in Houston, declared: "The work ethic is dead. Somewhere along the line, people have lost sight of pride in what they do. Kids no longer realize that whatever job they have it has some dignity."[15]

Young workers are also hampered by poor work habits. Many do not know what it means to come to work on time or how to cooperate with fellow workers, take supervision or separate per-

[12] Quoted in *Time*, Aug. 29, 1977, p. 15.
[13] Midge Decter, "Looting and Liberal Racism," *Commentary*, September 1977, p. 52.
[14] See, for example, Leonard Goodwin, *Do the Poor Want to Work: A Social-Psychological Study of Work Orientations* (1972), a study sponsored by the Brookings Institution which concluded that the poor value work as much as others in society, and that they lose interest in work only when they discover that their efforts do not lead to success.
[15] Quoted in *U.S. News & World Report*, May 9, 1977, p. 95.

sonal problems from the job. "The first time there is a hassle on the job, they just quit," said Ribnick. "This general lack of respect for anyone in authority is an attitude developed at home, passed to school and then to an employer."

This disdain for work and authority was one factor cited by apple growers in nine northeastern and mid-Atlantic states[16] in asking the Department of Labor to approve the importation of about 5,000 foreign workers, mainly Jamaicans, to harvest this fall's crop. The growers said they could not recruit enough American workers to do the job. A federal district court judge in Virginia agreed and, on Aug. 24, he ordered the department to admit the foreign workers. Some Labor officials, including Secretary Marshall, said the growers did not try hard enough to find domestic workers.

Federal Role in Job Creation

IT WAS NOT until the Depression years of the 1930s that the federal government assumed the burden of providing jobs for the nation's unemployed. Government concern was previously directed toward supplying employers with needed workers rather than assuring workers a sufficiency of jobs. Such measures as the establishment of land grant colleges[17] and provision of funds for vocational education reflected government interest in improving the skills of the nation's youth to meet the demands of technologically advancing agriculture and industry.

With the massive unemployment that followed the stock market crash of October 1929, the government's attention was forcibly turned to the problem of what to do with an idled labor force of unprecedented dimensions. When President Roosevelt took office on March 4, 1933, nearly 13 million persons—about one-fourth of the labor force—were out of work and looking for jobs. Because of the high level of adult unemployment, thousands of young people who normally would have gotten jobs on farms or in factories, stores and offices found most doors closed. "By 1933, 200,000 'wandering boys' were riding the freight trains in search of work or simply escape from a society that had no place for them."[18] They slept in shanty towns, in haystacks, on the floors of missions or jails. Robert Carter was one of the young men wandering around the country during the

---

[16] Virginia, West Virginia, New York, Vermont, Massachusetts, New Hampshire, Connecticut, Rhode Island and Maine.
[17] By the Morrill Act of 1862.
[18] *Life Magazine Special Report: The New Youth*, fall 1977, p. 45.

Depression, and he managed to put down some of what he did and saw in an article published in *The New Republic* on March 8, 1933.

> Leaving Macon I am the only one on the freight to Atlanta [Carter wrote]. Perhaps there are others, for this line has a bad name and we may be hiding from each other.... Forty miles from Atlanta the train stopped for water and the railroad detective found me and said I could ride no further—that I would be arrested in Atlanta anyway. I must have been a strange sight. My hair was long and billowed like rank vegetation beneath the dirty, once white, cap I wore....
>
> Leaving Atlanta with three other boys, youngsters going deeper South, we were rounded up in the railroad yards by five detectives carrying pistols and shotguns. They caught 18 or 20 of us after beating the bushes about the yards. They herded us to a bank beside the railroad, all of us young, none over 25 except a middle-aged man looking for a place by some river to jungle-up for the winter.... They herded us to the highways, took our names and told us if they caught us again it would be six months on the chain gangs....
>
> Was walking up a road when I met a new recruit to our ranks. He was a young farmer boy just leaving home, and he had a wild, vague look of pride and uneasiness at his venture. With his bundle and his unkempt clothes he was on his way to Texas, where he said he had heard they were paying three dollars a day for farmhands. We wished each other good luck and went on our way.[19]

Civilian Conservation Corps and NYA

To deal with the problems of unemployed youths, the Roosevelt administration devised two programs, the Civilian Conservation Corps and the National Youth Administration. The CCC put young[20] single men from families on public relief to work in forestry, flood control and similar projects. Roosevelt outlined the goals of the program in a message to Congress delivered March 21, 1933:

> The CCC [Roosevelt said] will conserve our precious natural resources. It will pay dividends to the present and future generations. More important, however...will be the moral and spiritual value of such work. The overwhelming majority of unemployed Americans...would infinitely prefer work. We can take a vast army of these unemployed out into healthful surroundings. We can eliminate to some extent at least the threat that enforced idleness brings to spiritual and moral stability. It is not a panacea for all unemployment but it is an essential step....

Reaction to Roosevelt's proposal was mixed. Some Cabinet members said that it might be dangerous to collect large groups

---

[19] Reprinted in *The Strenuous Decade: A Social and Intellectual Record of the Nineteen-Thirties,* edited by Daniel Aaron and Robert Bendiner (1970), pp. 45-52.
[20] Between the ages of 18 and 25, extended in 1935 to 17-28.

of jobless, and presumably resentful, young men in the woods. The labor movement said the plan would mean the militarization of labor and the reduction of wages to a subsistence level.

Despite the opposition, Congress approved the CCC legislation on March 31, 1933. By the middle of June, 1,300 CCC camps were established; by the end of July, more than 300,000 boys were enrolled. Over the next nine years, more than 2.5 million youths would spend from six months to a year in the program. Approximately 10 per cent of the CCC recruits were black, serving usually in segregated camps. In addition to food, shelter and military clothing, each person received $30 a month, most of which—$22 to $25—he was required to send home to his parents or other dependents. In exchange, the young men planted millions of trees; constructed roads, reservoirs and fish ponds; built terraces in eroded areas; restored historic battlefields; built bridges and fire towers; cleared beaches and camping grounds; and in a multitude of ways protected and improved parks, forests, watersheds and recreational areas. The value of the land improvements carried out by the CCC was estimated at $1.75-billion.[21]

The CCC program is believed to have had a tremendously beneficial effect on the participants, some of whom had never before been out of the city. Historian Arthur M. Schlesinger Jr. described the impact of the program: "The CCC participants [Schlesinger wrote] did more...than reclaim and develop natural resources. They reclaimed and developed themselves.... Their muscles hardened, their bodies filled out, their self-respect returned. They learned trades; more important, they learned about America, and they learned about other Americans."[22]

Although the work of the CCC is better remembered than that of the National Youth Administration, the latter at times employed larger numbers of people. Roosevelt created the NYA by executive order on June 26, 1935, to give public service jobs to out-of-school youngsters who could find no place in the shrunken job market. At the time the NYA was established, there were 2,827,000 young people, 16-24, out of work and out of school. By 1938, the NYA had 481,000 youngsters on its rolls, about evenly divided between boys and girls. The agency set up a special office of minority affairs, with a leading black educator, Mary McLeod Bethune, as director. In Texas, a local administrator was Lyndon B. Johnson.

NYA enrollees worked about 40 hours a month and received a

---

[21] Senate Labor Committee, "Report on Youth Conservation Act of 1959," p. 13.
[22] Schlesinger, *The Age of Roosevelt: The Coming of the New Deal* (1939), pp. 338-339.

monthly salary of $6 to $40. Most of them lived at home and, unlike CCC boys, had no distinctive uniform or insignia. They repaired highways, streets and public buildings; did clerical jobs; worked in libraries; constructed and landscaped parks; made maps and distributed health materials. In fact, their range of activities was immensely broad.[23] Between 1935 and 1943, some 2,667,000 young people participated in the NYA out-of-school work program. Close to 750,000 students in 1,700 colleges and universities and over 28,000 high schools received benefits through NYA student jobs.

Availability of Jobs During and After War

World War II brought an end to the lingering unemployment problems which the New Deal had been unable to solve. Both the Civilian Conservation Corps and the National Youth Administration were phased out during the war. More than 16,000,000 Americans—more than 10 per cent of the U.S. population—served in the armed forces during the war years, 1941-45.

American youths entering the job market during the 1940s and early 1950s had a relatively easy time finding work. The great economic expansion of the war and postwar years provided ample employment opportunities, except in brief periods of recession. Competition for jobs was reduced by the manpower demands of the military during the Korean War and by the opening of educational opportunities to veterans under the GI Bill. The job situation for youth changed in the late 1950s and early 1960s. The GI education program tapered off and the number of enlisted men fell from about three million in 1953, when the Korean War ended, to around two million in mid-1961.

Several other trends affected youth employment in the early 1960s.[24] Automation and other technological changes in industry led to the curtailment of some traditional entry-level jobs for young workers. At the same time employers began to tighten skill and education requirements. A high school diploma generally was required, and more employers looked for a college background. Opportunities for work on farms or in unskilled industrial jobs—areas in which one-fifth of all workers under 25 were employed in 1957—were declining. By May 1961, the unemployment rate for workers aged 16-20 was 17 per cent—two and a half times higher than the national average.

As is the situation today, the unemployment rate was highest among young blacks living in urban slums. Special surveys conducted for a 1961 conference on the problems of unemployed

---

[23] See Betty and Ernest K. Lindley, *A New Deal for Youth* (1938).
[24] See "Jobs for Young People," *E.R.R.*, 1961 Vol. II, pp. 499-517.

urban youth[25] showed that in one slum section, 59 per cent of the males between the ages of 16 and 21 were out of school, unemployed and "roaming the streets." In another ghetto area, 70 per cent of the boys and girls in that age group were neither in school nor at work. In an address to the conference, James B. Conant, president emeritus of Harvard University, described the consequences of these high unemployment rates. "The building up of a mass of unemployed and frustrated Negro youth in congested areas of a city," Conant said, "is a social phenomenon that may be compared to the piling up of inflammable material in an empty building.... Potentialities for trouble—indeed, possibilities of disaster—are surely there."

Controversy Over the Job Corps in 1960s

Conant's warning did not go unheeded. President Johnson made finding jobs for disadvantaged youths an important part of his war on poverty. At the center of Johnson's plan for improving the employment prospects of urban youths was the Job Corps, created as part of the Economic Opportunity Act of 1964. "Its avowed purpose was to take poor youths aged 16 to 21 years, to remove them from their debilitating poverty environments to distant residential centers, and there provide them with educational and vocational training needed to improve their employability."[26] By mid-1967, the Job Corps had 42,000 trainees enrolled in 123 centers around the country. A total of $989-million was allocated to the program during its first four years of operation.

From the first the Job Corps was controversial. Many questioned the basic premise of the program—that disadvantaged youngsters must be removed from their homes before they could be rehabilitated through training and education. Many of the centers were too big and were plagued by social tensions, partly because none of them was coeducational and many were placed in small towns and rural areas. There were a number of fights and shootings, which led to bad publicity. Critics said the training was costlier than a year at Harvard; it ran as high as $9,500 per trainee. Others questioned the program's effectiveness, pointing to the high dropout rate and the number of graduates who were unable to find jobs. According to Sar A. Levitan, "The Job Corps could have avoided a great deal of criticism and unfavorable publicity if the administration had decided to attract the 'cream' of the disadvantaged youth."[27]

---

[25] Conference on Unemployed, Out-of-School Youths in Urban Areas sponsored by the National Committee for Children and Youth in Washington, D.C., on May 24, 1961.

[26] Sar A. Levitan and Benjamin H. Johnston, *The Job Corps: A Social Experiment That Works* (1975), p. 1.

[27] Sar A. Levitan and Garth L. Mangum, *Federal Training and Work Programs in the Sixties* (1969), p. 166.

Instead the Job Corps concentrated on the most poorly educated, those who were least able to obtain jobs on their own.

Adding to the Job Corps' problems and its negative image was the continued increase in the proportion of black and other non-white enrollees—a factor which, according to Levitan, "contributed to the tensions experienced in the centers and to the early departure of some enrollees." During the first year of the program, whites constituted a majority of the Job Corps trainees. By July 1967, the ethnic distribution of Job Corps enrollment was 32.3 per cent Caucasian, 58.5 per cent black, and 9.2 per cent other minorities. Another continuing operational difficulty was the declining age of enrollees. By mid-1967 over half of the participants were 16 and 17 years old. Some local communities began to lobby for the closing of nearby local centers and in April 1969 President Nixon complied. He closed 59 centers around the country and cut the Job Corps budget from $280.5-million to $180.5-million, a level that prevailed until this year despite inflation *(see p. 85)*.

Implications for the Future

C ONTINUED HIGH LEVELS of youth unemployment have produced renewed interest in proposals to establish a separate, lower minimum wage for teenage workers. Supporters argue that a low wage is an incentive for employers to hire young, inexperienced workers. Without such an incentive, they say, employers are less willing to invest time and effort in training young workers. Opponents of a subminimum wage for teenagers fear that employers would be tempted to substitute lower-paid youths for adult workers. The House, on Sept. 15, narrowly defeated an amendment to the Minimum Wage Bill that would have permitted employers to pay teenage workers (below age 19) 85 per cent of the minimum wage for the first six months on the job. A similar proposal was defeated by the Senate on Oct. 7, but public debate on the issue is expected to continue.

Proponents of a separate youth wage point to several recent studies showing that past increases in the minimum wage have been followed by increases in teenage unemployment. Professor James F. Ragan Jr. of Kansas State University wrote in the May 1977 issue of Harvard's *Review of Economics and Statistics* that about 225,000 teenage jobs—equal to about 17 per cent of the teenage employment total—were lost after Congress voted in 1966 to raise the minimum wage by 28 per cent and expand its coverage. In a 1976 study prepared for the Brookings Institution,

Underemployment of College Graduates

Unskilled high school dropouts are not the only young people having trouble finding a job. Great numbers of college graduates are either unemployed or have taken jobs outside their chosen fields. This is especially true for liberal arts majors. Many are underemployed—working at jobs which traditionally did not require a college degree. Ivar Berg, a Columbia University economist, estimates that 80 per cent of the college graduates today are taking jobs that were once held by the less-educated. The spillover of college graduates into low-skilled jobs is pushing people without a degree further down the employment ladder.

Government statistics indicate that the situation will get worse before it gets better. The Bureau of Labor Statistics, in its most recent "Occupational Outlook for College Graduates," estimated that during the 1974-1985 period there would be 950,000 more college graduates than jobs that have traditionally required degrees. This surplus of college graduates "does not necessarily mean that college graduates will experience significant levels of unemployment," the bureau concluded. "Instead, problems for college graduates will center on underemployment and job dissatisfaction...."

The psychological impact of the current job crunch was described by Joel Kotkin, a Los Angeles writer: "In the past a man with training and an education knew that sooner or later his skills would be marketable. Today our growing surplus population, many with Ph.D.'s, wonder if they'll ever get a job. This feeling of being surplus, no longer necessary, plagues the generation of the '70s. They are bitter, anxious and harshly aware of the Darwinian economic struggle."*

*Human Behavior, May 1977.

economist Edward M. Gramlich of the University of Michigan estimated that there was a 13 per cent rise in teenage unemployment because of the 25 per cent boost in the minimum wage in 1974.[28]

Walter E. Williams, a well-known black economist from Temple University in Philadelphia, argues that the minimum wage should be abolished because it perpetuates discrimination against blacks and other minority youths.[29] Williams contends that they should have the right to enhance their employment prospects by charging less for their services. Rep. Parren J. Mitchell, chairman of the Congressional Black Caucus, disagrees. Noting the potential for displacement of adult workers by lower-paid youth, Mitchell told the House during debate on

---

[28] Edward M. Gramlich, "Impact of Minimum Wages on Other Wages, Employment and Family Incomes," *Brookings Papers on Economic Activity,* 1976, pp. 409-451.

[29] Walter E. Williams, "Government Sanctioned Restraints that Reduce Economic Opportunities for Minorities," *Policy Review,* fall 1977, preprint 2, p. 9.

the minimum wage bill: "Unemployment is chronic and endemic and deep across-the-board in the black community, and it does not make any sense to play one group of workers off against another."

Organized labor attacked the idea of a youth differential in the minimum wage as a thinly disguised way of assuring cheap labor. "Lowering wages does not create jobs, but it does create poverty," AFL-CIO President George Meany testified before the House Education and Labor Committee in August. Kenneth Young, the federation's associate director of legislation, argued that employers might be tempted to fire young workers after six months when the differential expired. Labor Secretary Marshall said at a press conference Aug. 31 that a subminimum wage for youth would have "catastrophic" effects on employment generally by substituting "white middle-class kids" for older workers, especially blacks. More effective in helping young blacks find employment, Marshall said, would be legislation to curb the flow of illegal aliens into this country, since illegal aliens compete most directly with young blacks for jobs.[30]

Some foes of the subminimum wage say the best solution to the teenage unemployment problem is a more vigorous economy that would create more jobs. They advocate enactment of the Humphrey-Hawkins bill,[31] requiring the federal government to reduce joblessness to 4 per cent within four years, through public service jobs if necessary. The measure also calls for comprehensive youth job programs and grants to local and state governments for job generation. First introduced in 1974, the bill has undergone numerous modifications. President Carter on Sept. 25 told a fund-raising dinner sponsored by the Congressional Black Caucus that he would try to work out differences with Congress and seek an acceptable draft version of the bill.

Different Views as to Problem's Severity

Experts disagree on the severity of the youth unemployment problem. Economist Richard B. Freeman of Harvard University said recently, "Teenage unemployment may be mainly a transitional problem without long-term consequences."[32] Those who think the problem has been overstated point to the special character of teenage unemployment. Teenagers tend to remain unemployed for shorter periods than adults and to change jobs more frequently. Many remain dependent on their families and are not seeking permanent or full-time employment. Others are experimenting with different kinds of jobs before they settle

---

[30] See "Illegal Immigration," *E.R.R.*, 1976 Vol. II, pp. 907-926.
[31] Named for its chief sponsors, Sen. Hubert H. Humphrey (D Minn.) and Rep. Augustus F. Hawkins (D Calif.).
[32] Quoted in *Business Week*, Oct. 10, 1977, p. 68.

down. "A youngster who is looking for a part-time job to earn enough to buy a stereo may be upset if he can't find work readily, and he certainly adds to the unemployment statistics," Freeman said. "But he is hardly going to suffer long-term damage."

A recent report on youth unemployment by the National Advisory Council on Vocational Education[33] declared that "the severity of the problem varies from mild to extreme." The council went on to say: "Many youths classified as 'unemployed' are sampling the labor market, and may be temporarily idle between jobs. Some youths who are out of work longer are from middle-income families, live at home, and do not suffer immediate economic hardship. For others, especially minorities, lack of employment can mean severe economic hardship and is often a matter of survival for themselves and their families."

Projected Decline in Teenage Population

Some experts say that time alone is needed to cure the problem. They point out that the last of the "baby boom" generation is entering adulthood and, consequently, the number of teenagers is starting to decline. The latest population projections by the Census Bureau[34] indicate a decline in the 14-17 age group in the years ahead, and, starting in 1980, in the 18-24 category as well, as is shown in the following table:

Years	Ages 14-17	Ages 18-24
1975-80	−7 %	+6.7%
1980-85	−8.7	−5.5

By 1990 the youth labor force is likely to total 21 million, about 1.3 million less than in 1975, according to Department of Labor projections. "By the end of the century, youth unemployment may not be an issue at all," the National Advisory Council on Vocational Education has concluded. "The issue may be, instead, the retraining of adult and retired persons to fill vacant job slots." George Iden, an economist with the Congressional Budget Office, has said that the teenage population decline could bring their jobless rate down by as much as 3.3 per cent by 1985.[35] But Iden went on to say that government youth employment programs may still be necessary because geography rather than demography is the key factor in minority-youth unemployment.

---

[33] "Youth Unemployment: The Need for a Comprehensive Approach," a report by the National Advisory Council on Vocational Education, March 1977, p. 1.
[34] U.S. Bureau of the Census, "Projections of the Population of the United States: 1977 to 2050," *Current Population Reports*, Series P-25, No. 704, 1977, p. 10.
[35] Quoted in *The New York Times*, Aug. 30, 1977.

Donald Eberly thinks it is "unlikely" that population changes will solve the youth job problem. "The decline in the youth population," he wrote,"may easily be more than compensated for by the continuing entry of women into the labor force." And, he went on to say, "It seems almost certain that many older people will extend their stay in the labor force." A bill that would raise the mandatory retirement age in private industry from 65 to 70 was approved Sept. 23 by the House but has encountered opposition in the Senate.

Even if population changes improve the job prospects of future generations of teenagers, the effects of the current job crunch are likely to be felt for a long time. For one thing, many young people have had to settle for low-level positions that are needed by the next wave of job seekers. As these "underemployed" workers pile up, said Princeton University sociologist Charles F. Westoff, more and more Americans will find career ladders blocked by a glut of senior employees. At that point, "our view of America as the land of opportunity is going to fade." Philip M. Hauser, director of the Population Research Center at the University of Chicago, has said that the fierce competition for jobs could lead to pressure for a welfare state. "What this all adds up to," he said, "is that you're going to have a huge generation for whom the American system has not worked."[36]

Whether current youth employment problems will have such consequences is unknown. What is certain is that there are no instant answers. But until the United States solves the youth unemployment problem the nation will continue to pay the price, in terms of higher welfare costs, a higher crime rate, and a growing number of embittered, alienated youths who may never find productive roles in society.

---

[36] Westoff and Hauser are quoted in *U.S. News & World Report*, Oct. 3, 1977, p. 55.

Selected Bibliography

Books

Goodwin, Leonard, *Do the Poor Want to Work? A Social-Psychological Study of Work Orientations,* the Brookings Institution, 1972.
Levitan, Sar A. and Benjamin H. Johnston, *The Job Corps: A Social Experiment That Works,* Johns Hopkins University Press, 1975.
—— and Garth L. Mangum, *Federal Training and Work Programs in the Sixties,* Institute of Labor and Industrial Relations, 1969.

Articles

"A Bitter New Generation of Jobless Young Blacks," *U.S. News & World Report,* Sept. 27, 1976.
Decter, Midge, "Looting and Liberal Racism," *Commentary,* September 1977.
Eccles, Mary Eisner, "Lower Minimum Wage Urged for Teenage Workers," *Congressional Quarterly Weekly Report,* Sept. 10, 1977.
—— "Congress Mounts Attack on Youth Unemployment," *Congressional Quarterly Weekly Report,* May 28, 1977.
"The Explosive Issue of Youth Unemployment," *Business Week,* Oct. 10, 1977.
"Why It's Hard to Cut Teenage Unemployment," *U.S. News & World Report,* May 17, 1976.
Williams, Walter E., "Government Sanctioned Restraints That Reduce Economic Opportunities for Minorities," *Policy Review,* fall 1977.
"Would the 'Teenwage' Cut Unemployment?" *Business Week,* Sept. 19, 1977.
Young, Anne McDougall, "Students, Graduates, and Dropouts in the Labor Market, October 1976," *Monthly Labor Review,* July 1977.
"Young People Without Jobs—How Real a Problem?" *U.S. News & World Report,* May 9, 1977.

Reports and Studies

American Enterprise Institute, "Minimum Wage Legislation," June 27, 1977.
Bureau of Labor Statistics, "Occupational Outlook for College Graduates, 1976-1977 Edition," 1977.
Editorial Research Reports, "Government Youth Corps," 1961 Vol. I, p. 1; "Jobs for Young People," 1961 Vol. II, p. 499; "Underemployment in America," 1975 Vol. II, p. 503.
National Advisory Council on Vocational Education, "Youth Unemployment: The Need for a Comprehensive Approach," March 1977.
National Child Labor Committee, "Rite of Passage: The Crisis of Youth's Transition from School to Work," 1976.
"The Job Crisis for Black Youth: Report of the Twentieth Century Fund Task Force on Employment Problems of Black Youth," Praeger, 1971.
U.S. Bureau of the Census, "Projections of the Population of the United States: 1977 to 2050," *Current Population Reports,* Series P-25, No. 704, 1977.

WOMEN IN THE WORK FORCE

by

Sandra Stencel

**Feb. 18
1977**

WOMEN IN THE WORK FORCE

RESPONDING TO changing views of their role in society and inflationary pressures on family budgets, women are surging into the U.S. labor force at an unprecedented rate. Not even in the World War II days of Rosie the Riveter did so many women work outside the home. Nearly half—47 per cent—of the American women 16 and older held jobs or were actively looking for work last year. Among women aged 20 to 64, the prime working year, the percentage was even higher. Over 56 per cent of the women in this group were employed.[1]

The number of American women who work has been rising steadily since 1947 (see box, p. 105). But during the last few years and especially in 1976, women entered the job market at a pace called "extraordinary" by Alan Greenspan, chairman of President Ford's Council of Economic Advisers.[2] Last year 1.6 million women entered the work force. Over the past 25 years the number of American working women more than doubled, rising to nearly 39 million in 1976 from just 19 million in 1951. The Bureau of Labor Statistics estimates that nearly 12 million more women will be added to the work force by 1990.[3] According to the same projection, the number of men in the labor force will grow by less than 10 million during that period. Although men are expected to continue to make up the larger part of the labor force, their participation is expected to continue its slow, long-term decline.

The Department of Labor, in its "1975 Handbook on Women Workers," labeled this increase in the number and proportion of women who work as "one of the most spectacular changes in the American economy in the past quarter-century." Eli Ginzberg, a Columbia University economist and chairman of the National Commission for Manpower Policy, called it "the single most outstanding phenomenon of our century," and he went on to say that "its long-range implications are absolutely unchartable."[4]

Some economists say that the influx of women—and also teenagers—into the labor force accounts for the nation's con-

---

[1] Statistics from U.S. Department of Labor, Bureau of Labor Statistics, "Employment and Earnings," Vol. 23, No. 5, November 1976, pp. 21-22.
[2] White House press conference, Sept. 3, 1976.
[3] Monthly Labor Review, October 1976, p. 2. The Monthly Labor Review is published by the Department of Labor.
[4] Quoted in The New York Times, Sept. 12, 1976.

tinued high unemployment rate. In 1976, the nation's unemployment rate fluctuated between 7.3 and 8.1. For both adult men and women, the rate was lower, but for teenagers it was far higher, as the following table illustrates:

Period	Overall Rate	Adult Women*	Adult Men*	Teen- agers
1976	7.7%	7.4%	5.9%	19.0%
1975	8.5	8.0	6.7	19.9
1974	5.6	5.5	3.8	16.0

* 20 and older

The primary cause of the current unemployment rate has not been people losing their jobs, John O'Riley of *The Wall Street Journal* wrote, but rather "the unprecedented number of new job seekers scrambling to get on the paycheck bandwagon." *Time* magazine commented that "the profound consequence" of women and teenagers entering the job market in large numbers "is that the number of people looking for work is leaping faster than the economy can provide jobs...."[5]

Feminists contend that such arguments ignore the economic reasons which force most women to seek work. "The only justification for those who, for political advantage, try to blame our high unemployment rate primarily on the spectacular influx of women into the labor force is that at least they have pinpointed a profound change in the labor force," wrote financial columnist Sylvia Porter last September. "Their argument is viciously sexist. Their explanation shrugs off the vital importance of the woman's paycheck to prosperity and to the standard of living of millions of households."[6]

Economic and Social Factors in the Upsurge

Like all complex social changes, the back-to-work movement has been shaped by many economic and cultural forces. Economic need is clearly one of them. "Women now work because they have to," said Arlene Kaplan Daniels, a Northwestern University sociologist. This was especially true for the 8.5 million single women in the labor force in 1975 and for the nearly seven million women workers who were divorced or separated from their husbands. Of all women in the work force, about one out of eight (12.3 per cent) was either divorced or separated, according to a recent report by Allyson Sherman Grossman, an economist with the Bureau of Labor Statistics.[7]

[5] *The Wall Street Journal,* Jan. 17, 1977, and *Time,* Nov. 1, 1976, p. 25.

[6] Sylvia Porter, writing in *The Washington Star,* Sept. 20, 1976.

[7] Allyson Sherman Grossman, "The Labor Force Patterns of Divorced and Separated Women," *Monthly Labor Review,* January 1977, pp. 48-53. Daniels was quoted in *Newsweek,* Dec. 6, 1976, p. 69.

Women in the Work Force

Year	Number (add 000)	Percentage of Adult Female Population*
1947	16,683	31.8
1951	19,054	34.7
1956	21,495	36.9
1961	23,838	38.1
1966	27,333	40.3
1971	32,132	43.4
1972	33,320	43.9
1973	34,561	44.7
1974	35,892	45.7
1975	37,087	46.4
1976	38,520	47.4

*Ages 16 and older

Source: U.S. Department of Labor

Economic need was also behind the sharp rise in the labor force participation of married women in recent years. Of the more than 21 million married women who were in the labor force in March 1975, approximately 26 per cent were married to men earning less than $10,000 a year. Nearly three million working women had husbands who were unemployed or unable to work.[8] As inflation has eroded real disposable income, many middle-class families have come to rely on wives' earnings to maintain their standard of living. Without a second paycheck, they would find it difficult—if not impossible—to buy a house or send their children to college.

A number of factors other than economic need and the rising divorce rate have contributed to the increased number of working women. These include: (1) more effective means of birth control and the trend toward fewer children; (2) the increased life expectancy of women; (3) the greater number of college-educated women; and (4) the widespread use of labor-saving devices in the home. Other factors are the expansion of the white-collar job market in which most women are employed, the increase in part-time employment opportunities, and legal action prohibiting job discrimination based on sex.

There has been a tremendous change in attitude toward working women in recent years, primarily as a result of publicity given to the woman's movement. "As recently as 10 years ago, a woman had to defend her position if she wanted to work," said Beatrice Buckley, editor of a new monthly magazine called

---

[8] U.S. Department of Labor, "Why Women Work," July 1976.

Working Woman. "Now you have only to go out and ask the nearest housewife what she does and she'll answer, 'Just a housewife.' "[9] A recent survey of teenage girls and young women conducted for the American Council of Life Insurance found that only one in four wanted to be a housewife.[10]

A Roper Poll for *Fortune* in 1936 indicated that only 15 per cent of the population believed "married women should have a full-time job outside the house." Another Roper Poll for the magazine 10 years later found that by a 5-3 ratio Americans thought that housewives had more interesting lives than women who held full-time jobs. By 1969 the national temper had changed, according to a Gallup Poll. By a 5-4 majority, the poll's respondents said there was nothing wrong with married women earning money in business and industry.

A Gallup Poll in March 1976 found that 68 per cent of those interviewed approved of working wives. A study conducted later in the year by *The Washington Post* and the Harvard University Center for International Affairs indicated that men favored careers for women by a 2-1 ratio, women by 4 to 3. However, a nationwide poll conducted by Research Analysis Corp. of Boston for *Newsday* found that nearly half of those it surveyed agreed with the statement, "If a man doesn't want his wife to take a job, she should respect his wishes."[11]

Widening Pay Gap Between Men and Women

Women's pay has increased significantly in recent years but not as fast as men's *(see graph, p. 107)*. Consequently the difference between men's and women's pay is wider today than it was 20 years ago, according to a report issued last October by the Women's Bureau of the Department of Labor titled "The Earnings Gap Between Women and Men." It also noted that women earned substantially less than men at the same level of education. In fact, the average woman college graduate earned less than the average male high school drop-out. The study found that women were overrepresented at the lower end of the pay scale as the following table illustrates:

Earning Group	Male	Female
$ 3,000-$4,999	36.6%	63.4%
5,000-6,999	41.9	58.1
7,000-9,999	59.3	40.7
10,000-14,999	83.1	16.9
15,000 and over	94.7	5.3

[9] Quoted in *Newsweek*, Dec. 6, 1976, p. 69.
[10] American Council of Life Insurance, "The Family Economist," Nov. 3, 1976.
[11] *Post*-Harvard poll appeared in *The Washington Post*, Sept. 28, 1976, and the Research Analysis Corp. poll in *Newsday*, June 15, 1976.

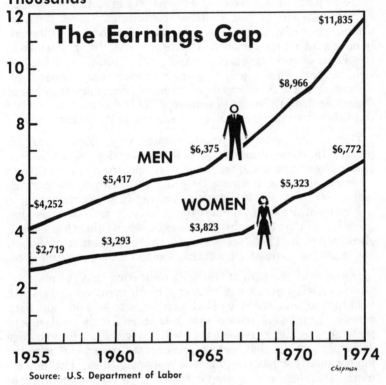

MEDIAN EARNINGS
Thousands

The Earnings Gap

$11,835

$8,966

$6,375

MEN

$6,772

$5,417

$5,323

$4,252

WOMEN

$3,823

$2,719 $3,293

Source: U.S. Department of Labor

Chapman

The widening wage gap between the sexes reflects the continued concentration of women in relatively low-skilled, low-paying jobs. According to the Department of Labor's "1975 Handbook on Women Workers," more than two-fifths of all women workers were employed in just 10 job categories in 1973: secretary, retail sales worker, bookkeeper, private household worker, elementary school teacher, waitress, typist, cashier, sewer and sticher, and registered nurse. Salaries were relatively low, averaging $4,700 for sales clerks and $6,400 for clerical workers. More than one-third of all women workers were employed in clerical jobs.

Helping to fill the clerical ranks are many college-educated women who cannot find other work. The Equal Employment Opportunity Commission estimates that 20 per cent of the college graduates who work are in clerical, semi-clerical or unskilled jobs. Economists say this is partly because many women major in the liberal arts and enter the job market with few marketable skills and partly because of discrimination. Businesses still tend to groom male college graduates for management jobs and women graduates for the secretarial pool.

Occupational segregation stems from many sources—discrimination, cultural conditioning, and the personal desires of women themselves. The jobs women traditionally have held are frequently related to the work they performed in the home—teaching children and young adults, nursing the sick, preparing food, assisting their husbands and other men. According to Dr. Nancy Smith Barret, an economics professor at American University in Washington, D.C., women have been conditioned to believe that these are the only "proper" jobs.[12]

During the period in which women were entering the job market in large numbers, jobs in the service industries, including health care and teaching, were opening up faster than in other occupations. Between 1964 and 1974, employment in the service industry nearly doubled. Another factor contributing to the concentration of women in the service industries is that part-time employment is more obtainable there than elsewhere.[13] In 1974, according to the Department of Labor, about 28 per cent of all working women held part-time jobs.

Despite the plethora of statistics indicating that the majority of women work because of economic need, many employers still hold to the traditional view that men ought to be paid more than women. Employers reason that men merit higher salaries or preference in hiring because they will not withdraw for marriage and childbearing; that men can give more time and effort to the job because they have no domestic responsibilities; that they are more valuable as employees because of their greater mobility; or that they need more money to support their families. Because they see women as temporary fixtures in the labor force many employers tend to shuttle women into jobs where the skills are quickly learned and there is little opportunity for advancement.

"The threat of discontinuity in a woman's worklife is perhaps the greatest single barrier to higher wages for young women," the new Secretary of Commerce, Juanita Kreps, wrote in her book *Sex in the Marketplace: American Women at Work* (1971). She added:

> The period of heaviest domestic responsibility occurs fairly early in a woman's worklife, when she is likely to be forced to make some quite long-range decisions: whether to acquire further job training, or additional formal education; how many children she will have; whether to continue working, at least part-time, during the childbearing period.... Her immediate job choice is dictated in large measure by the time constraint imposed in the short-run, and this choice in turn directs her subsequent career development.

---

[12] Quoted in *Redbook*, March 1975, p. 88.
[13] See article by Elizabeth Waldman and Beverly J. McEaddy, "Where Women Work—An Analysis by Industry and Occupation," *Monthly Labor Review*, May 1974, p. 3.

Because of their family responsibilities, many women prefer jobs that require little or no overtime work or traveling. One of the attractions of elementary school teaching for women is that they can coordinate their work with their children's schedules.

Shift to Professional and Blue-Collar Jobs

The pay gap does not disappear when women go into the professions. The median income for women college professors is 91 per cent that of their male colleagues. The average salary for women high school teachers is 81 per cent that of men. Female scientists earn 76 per cent as much as male scientists, and female engineers 85 per cent as much as their male counterparts. In some professions the situation for women is getting worse, not better. The latest figures from the National Center for Education Statistics in the Department of Health, Education and Welfare show that during the 1975-76 school year, the average salary for male faculty members rose faster than for females.

Almost 16 per cent of all women in the U.S. labor force are in the professions, mostly nursing and teaching. But growing numbers are seeking fuller access to such traditionally male-dominated professions as law, medicine, architecture, business and engineering. Today about 23 per cent of all law students in the United States are women, up from 8.5 per cent in 1971. The number of first-year women medical students has more than doubled since 1972.[14] About 25 per cent of all entering medical students are women, up from 11.3 per cent in 1970 and 8.9 per cent in 1965.

Among the nation's 1,300 biggest companies, *Business Week* reported Jan. 10, 1977, there are about 400 women directors versus about 20 just five years ago. However, these 400 represent only 2.7 per cent of the 15,000 board members of major corporations. More and more women are becoming junior executives and sales representatives, positions that often lead to the top. International Business Machines, which employed 400 women sales representatives in 1973, now has 1,400. At Xerox the percentage of women in the sales force has grown to 14.9, up from 1.7 in 1971. In other fields, too, women are starting to move up through the ranks. A recent report on commercial banking by the New York-based Council on Economic Priorities showed women making significant gains in managerial, professional, technical and sales posts.[15]

[14] See Mary Lynn M. Luy, "Status Report on Women in Medical Education: Up and Coming," *Modern Medicine,* Nov. 1, 1976, p. 33. The American Bar Association figure of 23 per cent is limited to women enrolled in ABA-approved law schools.

[15] The council found that between 1971 and 1975 the percentage of all bank managers and officials who were women jumped from 16 to 26. The number of women in professional, technical and sales categories climbed from 22 to 35 per cent. However, only 13 per cent of the bank officers and 1.8 per cent of the senior executives were women.

Women have made some inroads into blue-collar jobs that up until recently have been largely male enclaves. The signs of change are everywhere. From 1962 to 1975 the ratio of men to women changed from 70-1 to 20-1 among garage workers and gas station attendants, from 35-1 to 11-1 among mail carriers, and from 27-1 to 11-1 among taxicab drivers.[16] In Seattle, an organization called Mechanica has placed women as carpenters, machinists, diesel mechanics, laborers and truck drivers. Over 3,000 women were employed on the Trans-Alaska Oil Pipeline as craftsmen, clerks and cooks. Approximately 11,000 women make their living as carpenters and 700 women as coal miners.[17]

Despite these gains, the number of women who have cracked the sex barriers is relatively small, and the sight of women at the bottom of mines, at the top of telephone poles, and in the ranks of the police, firefighters and the military academies still draws the attention of the public and the news media. The Department of Labor, in its latest report on the subject, said that only 18 per cent of the total number of blue-collar workers were women at the end of 1975, about five million women in all.

History of Working Women in U.S.A.

V ERY FEW PEOPLE know that the official version of the Declaration of Independence, the one that was circulated to all the colonies, was printed by a woman—Mary Katherine Goddard of Baltimore. "The job of printing the Declaration went to a woman," author Caroline Bird wrote, "because as publisher of the leading newspaper in town, she had the facilities to do it."[18] In addition to being a successful newspaper publisher and printer, Mary Katherine Goddard was the new nation's first, and for many years the only, woman postmaster.

Although Mary Goddard was not typical of the women of her time, she was not unique either. Many colonial women were employed in the trades. Since most work was done at or near home, wives often assisted their husbands and frequently carried on the business if they were widowed. Many had come to the colonies as indentured servants and worked as domestic servants during their bondage. Other colonial women (especially

---

[16] Figures from Peter A. Morrison and Judith A. Wheeler, "Working Women and 'Woman's Work': A Demographic Perspective on the Breakdown of Sex Roles," The Rand Corporation, June 1976, p. 2.

[17] The Kentucky Commission on Human Rights has ordered a number of coal companies in the state to hire more women and wants women eventually to fill 20 per cent of the mining jobs in Kentucky. See *United Mine Workers Journal*, January 1977, p. 13.

[18] Caroline Bird, *Enterprising Women* (1976), p. 6.

widows) kept inns and taverns, managed retail businesses, and became seamstresses and milliners. The most important occupations for women during this period were spinning and weaving. At first most of this work was done at home. But as the demand for textiles increased, the factory system developed. By 1850, the textile mills of New England employed some 92,000 workers, two-thirds of them women.[19]

The earliest female mill operators were primarily the unmarried daughters of native Yankee farmers. Most of them worked in the mills only a few years before moving to marriage and occasionally school teaching. "Mill work was generally regarded as a desirable way to preserve young women from the moral perils of idleness," wrote Robert W. Smuts in his classic work *Women and Work in America* (1959). Between 1840 and 1860, Irish and French-Canadian immigrant women, many of them married, took over many of the mill jobs. Other immigrant women helped produce boots, shoes and cigars; toiled in printing plants and paper mills; or worked as housekeepers, chambermaids, charwomen, laundresses and cooks.

Civil War, Immigration and Labor Activity

The Civil War expanded the job opportunities for women, especially in office work, government service and retailing. Yet, in 1870, 70 per cent of the women who worked were still domestics. The average age of those employed was 23, and nearly 85 per cent were single and most contributed to the support of their families and lived with their parents. Their wages averaged $5.25 a week.

As immigrant women took over more of the industrial jobs, middle-class women began entering new occupations, such as teaching and social work. Mainly as a result of the Civil War, large numbers of women went into nursing and many stayed in the profession after the war. Despite these new opportunities, it was still rare for married women to work, especially in the middle classes, and even rarer for mothers to work. Among the four million working girls and women counted by the 1890 census, only half a million were married. A Bureau of Labor study of 17,000 women factory workers in 1887 found that only 4 per cent of them were married. Only one woman teacher out of 25 was married in 1890, partly because many communities would not hire married women. "Should a female teacher marry," declared the bylaws of New York City, "her place shall thereupon become vacant."[20]

By and large, married women worked only if their husbands

---

[19] Heidi I. Hartmann, "Women's Work in the United States" *Current History,* May 1976, p. 216.
[20] Cited in Robert W. Smuts' *Women and Work in America* (1959), p. 19.

were permanently or temporarily unable to support their families. Around the turn of the century, Smuts wrote, "When a married woman worked it was usually a sign that something had gone wrong." Only among blacks and the immigrant populations of New England textile towns was a large minority of wives employed outside the home. Among the blacks, according to the 1890 census, nearly one-fourth of the wives and nearly two-thirds of the widows were employed.

Partly because their options were so limited, many 19th century women eagerly embraced womanhood as a vocation in itself. The ideology of "True Womanhood," popularized through women's magazines such as *Godey's Lady's Book,* revolved around the notion that women's rightful place was in the home. However, this ideal was not readily attainable by most working-class women, who were more concerned with improving their working conditions.

Women industrial workers had formed local workingwomen's societies as early as the 1830s. "In the 1840s, women workers were in the leadership of labor militancy in the United States."[21] Women participated in attempts to form national unions in the 1860s and 1870s and in the Knights of Labor in the 1880s. At its height, the Knights of Labor had 50,000 women members—most of them organized into "separate but equal" locals. In 1886, the Knights hired the first woman investigator of female working conditions, Leonora Barry. But for the most part, women were discouraged from joining unions. "Keeping women out of the union was a way...to keep women out of the trade or to limit their participation."[22]

Nevertheless, women were active in the New England textile mill strikes conducted by the Industrial Workers of the World ("Wobblies") in 1912, and the AFL's International Ladies' Garment Workers Union began to organize vast numbers of women, many of them immigrants, in the needles trade in New York City in 1909. The tragic Triangle Fire in New York City in 1911, which killed 146 young women shirtmakers because the fire exits were locked, was a tremendous spur to organization. By 1920, the garment workers union had nearly 100,000 members.

Job Gains Coinciding With Push for Suffrage

World War I created new job opportunities for women, and thousands moved into jobs formerly held by men. Feminist leaders in the campaign for woman's suffrage were convinced that a new era of feminine equality was dawning. "Wonderful as

---

[21] Rosalynn Baxandall, Linda Gordon and Susan Reverby, eds., *America's Working Women* (1976), p. 66.
[22] *Ibid.*, pp. 83-84.

Women's Share
of the U.S. Labor Force

1990*	43%	1955	31%
1976	41	1950	29
1970	38	1940	25
1965	35	1930	22
1960	33	1920	20

* Projected
Source: U.S. Department of Labor

this hour is for democracy and labor," Margaret Drier Robbins told the Women's Trade Union League in 1917, "it is the first hour in history for the women of the world.... At last, after centuries of disabilities and discrimination, women are coming into the labor and festival of life on equal terms with men."[23]

But it was not to be. After the war both employers and male employees assumed that women would happily relinquish the new jobs and skills that they had acquired. The male-dominated AFL unions led the fight for legislation to exclude women from such jobs they had held during the war as meter reading, streetcar conducting, taxi driving and elevator operating; they were also excluded from night work and overtime, which effectively eliminated them from fields like printing.

Despite these restrictions, more women were working than ever before. During the 1920s the female labor force grew to 10.7 million from 8.4 million, a 26 per cent increase. Single women of the middle classes were entering clerical and sales work in in-

[23] Quoted in William Henry Chafe, *The American Working Woman: Her Changing Social, Economic and Political Roles, 1920-1970* (1972), p. 49.

creasing numbers. "Even the girls who knew that they were going to be married pretended to be considering important business positions," Sinclair Lewis wrote in his 1920 novel, *Main Street.* Frederick Lewis Allen noted in *Only Yesterday* (1931), his account of the 1920s, that after passage of the suffrage amendment in 1919 middle-class girls "poured out of schools and colleges into all manner of occupations," But according to William Henry Chafe, historians have overstated the amount of economic change which occurred in the decade.

> There is no evidence that a revolution took place in women's economic role after World War I, nor can it be said that the 1920s represented a watershed in the history of women at work.... Aspiring career women were still limited to positions traditionally set aside for females; the overwhelming majority of American working women continued to toil at menial occupations for inadequate pay; and the drive to abolish economic discrimination enlisted little popular support.[24]

The number of married women entering the labor force steadily increased. By 1940, 17 per cent of all women who worked were married. Still many people continued to oppose married women working, particularly during the Depression. The Gallup Poll in 1936 found that 82 per cent of the population objected. In the late 1930s bills were introduced in 26 state legislatures to keep married women from holding jobs. Only one of these passed. This was in Louisiana, and it was later repealed.

Breakthrough in the World War II Job Market

World War II had profound effects on the U.S. economy, and particularly on women workers. As millions of men went into uniform, women went into industry as never before, accounting for 36 per cent of the nation's labor force in 1945, up from 25 per cent in 1940. Wages rose, the number of wives holding jobs doubled and unionization of women quadrupled. Employers' attitudes toward women remained skeptical, but since women were the only available labor, they were hired.

Black women found jobs in manufacturing for the first time. Previous bans on the employment of married women were discarded; by 1944, married women comprised almost half of the female labor force. The war gave women access to more skilled and higher-paying jobs. Although the war made rapid changes in women's economic status, it did not make a lasting or profound difference in the public attitude toward working women, nor did it lead to greater equality between the sexes. Women continued to receive less pay than men (65 per cent less in manufacturing), to be denied opportunities for training and advancement, and to work in separate job categories. During the

[24] Chafe, *op. cit,* p. 51.

war, concluded William Henry Chafe, "traditional attitudes toward women's place remained largely unchanged."[25]

After the war, women were expected to return to their traditional role of homemaker. Behind the efforts of employers, educators, social workers and the media to persuade women to leave the work force were two important economic considerations, said the editors of *America's Working Women:* "On the one hand, the system could not provide full employment; on the other hand, continued industrial profits required, with the diminution of military spending, an expansion in the consumption of household durable goods. An emphasis on 'homemaking' encouraged women to buy."[26]

This view overlooked the fact that the majority of women were working for economic reasons. A Department of Labor survey in 1945 found that 96 per cent of all single women, 98 per cent of the widowed and divorced women, and 57 per cent of the married women seriously needed to continue working after the war. Many women were laid off in the heavy industries. But for the most part, these women did not return to their kitchens. Instead, they found work in the traditional areas still available to them. These were the only options open to many women until the 1960s, when anti-discrimination legislation opened up new opportunities.

Laws Banning Discrimination in Employment

Laws dealing with sex discrimination in employment have been enacted on both the federal and state levels in the past 15 years, beginning with the federal Equal Pay Act of 1963. It required all employers subject to the Fair Labor Standards Act[27] to provide equal pay for men and women performing similar work. In 1972, coverage of this act was extended to executives, administrators and professionals, including all employees of private and public educational institutions.

The courts have held that jobs do not have to be identical, only "substantially equal," for the Equal Pay Act to apply. In a well-publicized case involving the Corning Glass Works, the Supreme Court ruled in 1974 that shift differences (with men working at night and women working during the day) did not make the working conditions of the men and women dissimilar and thus would not justify a higher wage for the men.[28]

---

[25] Chafe, *op. cit.*, p. 188. See also Lyn Goldfarb, "Separated & Unequal: Discrimination Against Women Workers After World War II (The U.A.W. 1944-54)," The Women's Work Project, 1976.

[26] Rosalyn Baxandall, et al., *op. cit.*, pp. 282-283.

[27] The Fair Labor Standards Act of 1938 established a minimum wage for individuals engaged in interstate commerce or the production of goods for commerce. The law has been amended from time to time to increase the minimum rate and to extend coverage to new groups of employees.

[28] *Corning Glass Works v. Brennan*, 417 U.S. 188 (1974).

A milestone in equal employment opportunity for women was reached with the passage of the Civil Rights Act of 1964. Title VII of that act prohibited discrimination based on sex—as well as race, religion and national origin—in hiring or firing, wages and salaries, promotions or any terms, conditions or privileges of employment. Exceptions were permitted only when sex was a bona fide occupational qualification, as in the case of an actor or a wet nurse. Title VII is administered by the Equal Employment Opportunity Commission, whose five members are appointed by the President. Initially, the powers of the EEOC were limited largely to investigation and conciliation, but Congress amended the act in 1972 to let the agency go directly to court to enforce the law. The 1972 amendments also provided that discrimination charges could be filed by organizations on behalf of aggrieved individuals, as well as by employees and job applicants themselves.

Because sex discrimination sometimes took forms different from race discrimination, the EEOC issued sex-discrimination guidelines. They stated that the refusal to hire an individual cannot be based on assumed employment characteristics of women in general, and that the preferences of customers or existing employees should not be the basis for refusing to hire an individual. The guidelines also prohibited hiring based on classification or labeling of "men's jobs" and "women's jobs," or advertising under male and female headings.

The EEOC guidelines declared that state laws that prohibited or limited the employment of women—in certain occupations, in jobs requiring the lifting or carrying of specified weights, for more than a specified number of hours, during certain hours of the night, and immediately before and after childbirth—discriminate on the basis of sex because they do not take into account individual capacities and preferences. A series of court cases upheld this guideline, and according to the Bureau of Labor's "1975 Handbook on Women Workers," the conflict between state and federal laws on this point "was for the most part resolved in the early 1970s." In a case involving the guidelines, the Supreme Court ruled in 1971[29] that discrimination need not be intentional to be unlawful.

In October 1967, President Johnson issued an executive order barring sex discrimination and other forms of bias in hiring by federal contractors. Executive Order 11246 required federal contractors to take "affirmative action to ensure that applicants are employed and that they are treated during employment without regard to their race, color, religion, sex or national origin."[30]

---

[29] *Griggs et al. v. Duke Power Co.*, 401 U.S. 424 (1971).

[30] See "Reverse Discrimination," *E.R.R.*, 1976, Vol. II, pp. 561-580. See also *Affirmative Action For Women* (1975), by Dorothy Jongeward and Dru Scott.

Working Wives

The age of the two paycheck family has arrived. Since 1960, the number of families in which both husband and wife work has jumped to 42 per cent from 29 per cent. In 1976 alone an additional one million wives joined their husbands in the work force, according to the Department of Labor. The prime reason for their working was to help keep up with family bills.

During the 1950s the largest increase in labor force participation was among married women beyond the usual childbearing years (20 to 34). In recent years, however, there has been a sharp upturn in labor force participation of young married women, especially among married women with small children. Of the 21.1 million wives in the work force in March 1975, over half—11.4 million—had children under 18 years of age.

Why the dramatic upturn in working mothers? Perhaps one reason is that economists now estimate that it costs between $70,-000 and $100,000 to raise a child for the first 18 years of his or her life.*

*Reported by the Association of American Colleges in "Project on the Status and Education of Women," October 1976.

Other federal laws, orders and regulations have prohibited employment discrimination in special occupations or industries. For example, Title IX of the Education Amendments of 1972[31] specifically prohibited sex discrimination in education. Other laws and rules required affirmative action for minorities and women in construction and maintenance of the Alaska Pipeline.

The campaign to wipe out sex discrimination has resulted in court decisions and out-of-court settlements costing employers hundreds of millions of dollars in back pay and other benefits. Perhaps the most significant settlements were the two that the EEOC arranged with American Telephone & Telegraph Co. The first, signed January 1973, applied mostly to women and also to minority-group males who had been denied equal pay and promotion opportunities in non-management jobs. The agency ordered AT&T to award them $15-million in back pay and up to $23-million in pay increases. The second settlement, filed in May 1974, provided similar awards to management employees who were victims of illegal sex discrimination in pay. "The AT&T decision was important for symbolic reasons...," said Isabel Sawhill, a labor-market economist at the Urban Institute in Washington. "It established that companies have to look at their patterns of employment."[32]

---

[31] Amendments to the Higher Education Act of 1965, the Vocational Education Act of 1963, the General Education Provisions Act, and the Elementary and Secondary Education Act of 1965.
[32] Quoted in *Newsweek*, Dec. 16, 1976, p. 69. Other big cases subsequently have involved the Bank of America and the brokerage firm of Merrill Lynch.

Continuing Fight for Job Equality

DESPITE THESE VICTORIES, there still is widespread discrimination against women in the workplace. Many feminists say the problem lies not with the anti-discrimination laws and regulations, but with the enforcement efforts of the Equal Employment Opportunity Commission. The General Accounting Office, an investigative arm of Congress, reported recently: "Although the EEOC has had some success in obtaining relief for victims of discrimination in specific instances, it does not appear to have yet made the substantial advances against employment discrimination which will be necessary to make a real difference in the employment status of minorities and women."[33]

The backlog of discrimination complaints has risen to nearly 130,000, according to *The Washington Post*, Feb. 6, 1977. Workers who file complaints frequently wait years even to be told whether their charges have merit. By then, the worker may have given up and found other employment. The General Accounting Office said that nearly half (47.7 per cent) of the cases completed by the EEOC between July 1, 1972, and March 31, 1975, were "administrative closures," meaning that the worker could no longer be found or had lost interest in pursuing the charge. Only 11 per cent of the cases resolved during that period involved successfully negotiated settlements. According to the General Accounting Office, an individual has only one chance in 33 of having the charge settled successfully in the year it is filed. The average case takes nearly two years to settle.

In its 11-year history, the agency has had six successive chairmen and 10 executive directors. Not one chairman has completed his full five-year term. The position has been vacant since May 1976, when Lowell W. Perry resigned after one year in office. The agency's acting director, Ethel Bent Walsh, an EEOC commissioner since 1971, counts it as a sign of progress that the commissioners now meet and discuss problems. "When I first came here we didn't even talk to each other unless we met in the hall," she told the *Post*.

Dissension among the five commissioners may be inherent in the structure of the commission, according to Eleanor Holmes Norton, head of the New York City Commission on Equal Opportunity. "A commission structure involving five highly paid

---

[33] "The Equal Employment Opportunity Commission Has Made Limited Progress in Eliminating Employment Discrimination," Report to the Congress by the Comptroller General of the United States, Sept. 28, 1976.

presidential appointees, as EEOC now has, assumes that *policy* as opposed to *operational questions* will predominate," she said recently. "Administering an already unwieldy ship with what at times are five captains must be especially difficult in a period when operational problems are out of hand."[34] Her suggestion for improving EEOC operations—abolish the commission and appoint a single boss.

Other criticism has been directed toward the EEOC staff. In a recent article in *Fortune* magazine, Dorothy Rabinowitz accused the agency of being biased toward blacks at the expense of women and other minorities.[35] One reason for the agency's possible bias in favor of blacks, said Robert Ellis Smith, a former civil rights executive at the Department of Health, Education and Welfare, is that many of the senior positions are filled with alumni of the southern civil rights battles.[36] Acting Director Walsh told a House subcommittee in 1975 that many of the complaint investigators were "not of the caliber we required and have insufficient training." The National Commission on the Observance of International Women's Year in 1976 recommended that the EEOC "make a substantial effort to upgrade the quality of training of its personnel.[37]

Attempt to Nullify Court Ruling on Pregnancy Pay

Women's rights groups and organized labor plan to lobby this year for legislation to ensure sick pay for working women on leave because of pregnancy and thus counteract a recent Supreme Court ruling. The court held, on Dec. 7, 1976, that General Electric could exclude pregnancy from its employee disability insurance benefits without violating the 1964 Civil Rights Act. Writing for the court's 6-3 majority, Justice William H. Rehnquist said the exclusion was not discriminatory because "there is no risk from which men are protected and women are not...." In dissent, Justice William J. Brennan Jr.[38] wrote: "Surely it offends common sense to suggest...that a classification revolving around pregnancy is not, at the minimum, strongly 'sex related.' "

The business community generally applauded the decision. It saved American business $1.6-billion, the American Society for Personnel Administration estimated. In contrast, Karen

---

[34] Quoted by Robert Ellis Smith in "The EEOC and How to Make it Work," *Ms.* February 1977, p. 64. See also "A Look at What is Happening in Fight on Job Discrimination," *U.S. News & World Report*, Dec. 13, 1976, pp. 35-36.

[35] Dorothy Rabinowitz, "The Bias in the Government's Anti-Bias Agency," *Fortune*, December 1976, p. 138.

[36] Smith, *op. cit.*, p. 103.

[37] "To Form a More Perfect Union: Justice for American Women," Report of the National Commission on the Observance of International Women's Year, June 1976, p. 192. Walsh made her comments before the House Appropriations Subcommittee on State, Justice, Commerce, the Judiciary and Related Agencies on May 6, 1975.

[38] Also dissenting were Justices Thurgood Marshall and John Paul Stevens in the case, *General Electric v. Gilbert*, 429 U.S. 1976.

DeCrow, president of the National Organization for Women, called the ruling a "slap in the face to motherhood," and added, "If people are paid sick leave when they're out for nose jobs, hair transplants and vasectomies, why not for childbirth?"[39] In addition to lobbying for legislative remedies, union representatives plan to push for collective bargaining agreements with large employers that would ensure disability pay for women during pregnancy. It is estimated that 40 per cent of all U.S. companies have disability plans, and approximately 40 per cent of those include some maternity benefits.

Most criticism of the EEOC has focused on the backlog of cases. Initially it was thought that no more than 2,000 complaints a year would be filed, but in fiscal 1976 alone 75,173 were filed. Contributing to the agency's inability to cope with the growing number of complaints was a policy change in 1968. That year the agency began shifting much of its staff away from processing individual complaints in order to undertake broad investigations into widespread discriminatory patterns of certain corporations and industries. Some say the EEOC should abandon the case-by-case approach altogether. But many feminists oppose this idea. "The whole purpose of Title VII," said Judith Lichtman of the Women's Legal Defense Fund, "was to remove the burden from individual employees and make the government investigate complaints." Perry, the former commissioner, wonders whether the EEOC ought not to be abolished entirely and its responsibilities turned over to the Justice Department. But the agency's supporters credit it with fostering an atmosphere that encourages job equity.

Psychic Barriers to Women's Advancement

In many instances the barriers to women are not overt discrimination. Psychologists say working women are frequently handicapped by a weak self-image and lack of confidence. In a classic study in 1968, psychologist Matina Horner, now president of Radcliffe College, concluded that as a result of their childhood training and various social pressures of home and family, many women are hobbled by a "fear of success"—an acquired fear that the risks of succeeding are "loss of femininity."

The reasons for the absence of women in top management positions go beyond the "fear of success" syndrome, according to Margaret Hennig and Anne Jardim, co-directors of the Simmons College graduate program in management. They found that women's attitudes toward work are totally different from men's and that this impedes women's progress in the male-dominated corporate world. Men, they said, tend to have long-term career goals, while women are likelier to focus on short-

[39] Quoted in *The New York Times*, Dec. 16, 1976.

The Secretary Trap

An experiment conducted recently at the University of Maryland demonstrated the tendency of employers to shunt women into secretarial jobs. Male and female students, all white so that racial bias would not enter the picture, and all equally qualified, applied for jobs at 39 employment agencies.

Seventy-seven per cent of the men and 59 per cent of the women received job offers. Among the men, nine of ten job offers were for administrative or managerial positions and the rest were clerical. For the women, 82 per cent were clerical and 17 per cent were managerial. All of the women applicants were asked to take typing tests. The men were interviewed about their interests, ambitions and favorite sports.

term planning, largely because they have been brought up to think of careers conditionally—as an alternative to marriage. This ambiguity causes women to make their career decisions late, about the age of 30 to 33, while men generally build the foundations of their careers while they are still in their twenties.

Women are further hindered, according to Hennig and Jardim, by their lack of exposure to the informal factors that govern a man's world—contacts built up through clubs and golf games, or "old boy" relationships often started in college. "In the competition for career advancement...men have a clear advantage over women."[40] To help women overcome some of these disadvantages, some employers are encouraging their female employees to attend assertiveness training courses and other programs designed to enhance their self-image.

Changing women's attitudes may take some time. But there are other factors hindering women's participation in the labor force. One-third of the working women have children to care for. There are 6.5 million children under the age of 6, and 18 million others 6 to 14, whose mothers work. Yet according to the latest government estimates, care in licensed day-care centers is available for only slightly more than one million children.[41]

The burdens of child care for working mothers are compounded by other household responsibilities. Although men are doing more of the child rearing and housework these days, the women still bear the brunt of it. Despite all the difficulties, working women show no signs of abandoning their new roles in the work force. However, more and more working women are demanding that society and their families adjust to the new realities of women's lives.

[40] Margaret Hennig and Anne Jardim, "Women Executives in the Old-Boy Network," *Psychology Today*, January 1977, p. 81.
[41] See "Child Care," *E.R.R.*, 1972 Vol. I, pp. 441-460, and "Single-Parent Families," *E.R.R.*, 1976 Vol. II, pp. 661-680.

Selected Bibliography

Books

Baxandall, Rosalyn, Linda Gordon and Susan Reverby, *America's Working Women*, Vintage Books, 1976.

Bird, Caroline, *Born Female: The High Cost of Keeping Women Down*, Pocket Books, 1971.

——*Enterprising Women*, New American Library, 1976.

Chafe, William Henry, *The American Woman: Her Changing Social, Economic and Political Roles, 1920-1970*, Oxford University Press, 1972.

Jongeward, Dorothy and Dru Scott, *Affirmative Action for Women*, Addison-Wesley, 1975.

Kreps, Juanita, *Sex in the Marketplace: American Women at Work*, The Johns Hopkins Press, 1971.

Smuts, Robert W., *Women and Work in America*, Schocken, 1959.

Articles

"A Powerful New Role in the Work Force," *U.S. News & World Report*, Dec. 8, 1975.

Cowley, Susan Cheever, "Women at Work," *Newsweek*, Dec. 6, 1976.

Hartmann, Heidi I., "Women's Work in the United States," *Current History*, May 1976.

Hennig, Margaret and Anne Jardim, "Women Executives in the Old-Boy Network," *Psychology Today*, January 1977.

Kron, Joan, "The Dual Career Dilemma," *New York*, Oct. 25, 1976.

Rabinowitz, Dorothy, "The Bias in the Government's Anti-Bias Agency," *Fortune*, December 1976.

Smith, Robert Ellis, "The Equal Employment Opportunity Commission and How to Make It Work," *Ms*, February 1977.

"Women of the Year: Great Changes, New Chances, Tough Choices," *Time*, Jan. 5, 1976.

Reports and Studies

Editorial Research Reports, "Child Care," 1972 Vol. II, p. 439; "Single-Parent Families," 1976 Vol. II, p. 661; "Status of Women," 1970 Vol. II, p. 565.

Goldfarb, Lyn, "Separated and Unequal: Discrimination Against Women Workers After World War II (The U.A.W. 1944-1954)," The Women's Work Project, 1976.

Morrison, Peter A. and Judith P. Wheeler, "Working Women and 'Woman's Work': A Demographic Perspective on the Breakdown of Sex Roles," The Rand Corporation, June 1976.

"The Equal Employment Opportunity Commission Has Made Limited Progress in Eliminating Employment Discrimination," General Accounting Office, Sept. 28, 1976.

U.S. Department of Labor, "The Earnings Gap Between Women and Men," October 1976.

—— "U.S. Working Women: A Chartbook," 1975.

—— "Why Women Work," July 1976.

—— "Women Workers Today," October 1976.

—— "1975 Handbook on Women Workers," 1975.

ILLEGAL IMMIGRATION

by

Richard C. Schroeder

Dec. 10
1976

Editor's Note: The most significant response of the Carter administration to illegal immigration came on Aug. 4, 1977, when the President proposed a three-part plan to Congress: (1) Civil fines up to $1,000 for employers who knowingly hire illegal aliens; (2) intensive enforcement along the U.S.-Mexican border; and (3) eventual citizenship for persons who came illegally to the United States before 1970 and have continued to live here since then, and "temporary resident alien" status for others who can prove U.S. residence only since Jan. 1, 1977.

The proposed legislation remained in the Judiciary committees of the House and Senate when the 1977 session of Congress adjourned. There was disagreement between the two committees over whether civil or criminal penalties should be applied to U.S. employers who knowingly hire illegal aliens.

ILLEGAL IMMIGRATION

C HANGES IN U.S. immigration law due to take effect Jan. 1 will impose the most severe restrictions in history on legal immigration into the United States from other countries of the Western Hemisphere. For the first time, each of these countries will have a quota of 20,000 U.S.-bound emigrants each year. In addition, a preference system already in effect for the Eastern Hemisphere will be applied in this part of the world. The preferences favor close relatives of U.S. residents, refugees, and professionals and skilled workers.

The changes are intended to put the residents of this hemisphere on an equal footing with the rest of the world. Ironically the changes are expected to worsen, rather than ease, this nation's mounting immigration woes, especially the problems caused by the tide of illegal aliens. Illegal immigration into the United States has been increasing rapidly throughout the past decade. In 1965, the Immigration and Naturalization Service (INS) apprehended 110,371 illegal aliens; 1974 apprehensions had increased sevenfold to 788,145. In 1975, the total declined slightly to 766,600. By far the largest number of illegal aliens were clandestine border crossers, called EWIs (Entered Without Inspection) by the Immigration Service. In 1975, 87 per cent of those apprehended were EWIs. Other categories included visitors who had overstayed their visas, crewmen who had jumped ship, and students who had taken jobs or violated other provisions of their entry permits.

In the past several years, according to a study recently conducted for the Department of Labor, there has been an "explosive increase" in the amount of immigration—both legal and illegal—from Mexico and other countries of the Western Hemisphere.[1] Current immigration law permits 120,000 persons from this hemisphere to enter the country each year as resident aliens. Many times that number apply for admission. As a result, Latin American applicants face waiting periods of up to three years or more before gaining admission to the United States. In addition, many prospective immigrants must secure certification from the Department of Labor that they are not

---

[1] David S. North and Marion F. Houston, *"The Characteristics and Role of Illegal Aliens in the U.S. Labor Market: An Exploratory Study,"* March 1976, p. s-4.

likely to displace U.S. residents from their jobs. Because of the difficulty of immigrating legally, millions of Mexicans, West Indians and Canadians enter and stay in this country by clandestine methods.

The new provisions of the immigration law, signed by President Ford on Oct. 20, retain the overall hemispheric quota of 120,000, but limit immigration from each country to 20,000. Under the old law, hemispheric immigration was on a first-come, first-served basis, with no individual country limitation. Mexican legal immigration, for example, has been averaging 40,000 a year and reached a high of 70,000 in 1973. The national quota of 20,000 will cut legal immigration from Mexico in half and will inevitably increase the pressure for illegal entry. Similarly, more residents of Canada, Central America and the Caribbean, frustrated by the stiffer entrance tests, may be expected to enter the country illegally across the border or through Puerto Rico and the U.S. Virgin Islands, or to enter on a visitor's visa and go underground.

The vast majority of illegal immigrants in the United States already are from Latin America. A study conducted in 1975 for the Immigration Service[2] indicated that 8.2 million persons were in this country illegally. Of these, 5.2 million were from Mexico. Among the illegal aliens apprehended that year by the Immigration Service, an even larger proportion were from this hemisphere (94.8 per cent) and Mexico accounted for the lion's share (88.8 per cent).[3] One reason for the exceptionally large number of Mexicans is that the Immigration Service concentrates its personnel along the U.S.-Mexican border.

Effect on Labor Market and Economy of Nation

Despite numerous studies and surveys, no one can say precisely how many illegal immigrants are in the United States. In the past the Immigration Service estimated the total at between 4 million and 12 million. Last June, INS Commissioner Leonard F. Chapman Jr. revised this estimate to between 6 million and 8 million, and said that the number was growing by half a million a year.[4] What is reasonably certain is that the number of persons who enter the country illegally each year greatly exceeds the number of legal immigrants. In 1975, the INS admitted 386,194 legal immigrants and apprehended twice that number. An additional 800,000 persons were turned away at ports of entry. For every illegal entrant it detains, the Immigration Service estimates that four or five may elude capture.

---

[2] Lesko Associates, "Basic Data and Guidelines Required to Implement a Major Illegal Alien Study during Fiscal Year 1976," Immigration and Naturalization Service, Oct. 15, 1976. Lesko Associates ia a management consulting firm in Washington, D.C.

[3] Immigration and Naturalization Service, *1975 Annual Report.*

[4] Address to the Michigan Associated Press Editorial Association, June 11, 1976.

Whatever the true number of illegal immigrants in this country, their impact on the economy is substantial. Three-quarters of them come in search of jobs.[5] Most of the jobs they find are low paying and require few skills; they are likely to become janitors, busboys and farm workers. But a substantial number do find better jobs. Commissioner Chapman estimates that 3.5 million are employed in the United States, and that at least one million hold jobs that might otherwise be filled by un-employed Americans. At a time when 7.8 million Americans are out of work and the national unemployment rate stands at 8.1 per cent,[6] the impact of illegal immigration on the labor force cannot be dismissed lightly. According to the AFL-CIO, illegal aliens siphon off some $10-billion in wages each year from U.S. citizens and legal residents.[7]

There is some evidence that illegal aliens are less likely to avail themselves of welfare and food stamps than U.S. citizens and legal resident aliens with similar incomes.[8] Nonetheless, an independent study conducted for the Immigration Service in 1975 indicated that illegal aliens cost taxpayers $13-billion or more annually for public services such as health, education and sanitation. In addition, those employed in this country often are responsible for the support of families back home. The balance-of-payments loss attributable to remittances overseas by illegal aliens has been estimated at between $3-billion and $10-billion a year.

There is another side to the coin, of course. Illegal aliens are as much victims as culprits. Many work at jobs that pay less than the federal minimum wage and they dare not complain lest they be detected and deported. The recent study done for the Labor Department found that 20 to 25 per cent of the 793 illegal aliens studied "appear[ed] to have been paid below the minimum wage." The lowest paid workers were concentrated in agricultural occupations near the Mexican border.

The presence of illegal aliens in the labor force is said to depress wage levels for all other workers and to retard the rate of productivity improvement. In the case of productivity, growth declines not because illegal immigrants are poor workers but because their employers are unlikely to invest in labor-saving technology. Instead, inefficiencies in the production process are shifted to the workers in terms of lower pay.[9] Trade unions are ambivalent in their attitudes toward the illegal alien. On the one hand, they are concerned about the potential for lowering

---

[5] North and Houston, *op. cit.*, p. 66.
[6] Figures for November 1976, reported by the U.S. Bureau of Labor Statistics.
[7] Cited in John E. Karkashian, *The Illegal Alien*, Senior Session in Foreign Policy, Eighteenth Session, Department of State, 1976.
[8] North and Houston, *op. cit.*, p. 142.
[9] National Council on Employment Policy, *"Illegal Aliens: An Assessment of the Issues,"* October 1976, p. 11.

wages. On the other hand, since some illegals do join trade unions, union officials are obligated to protect them, as members, from exploitation and unfair labor practices.

Implications for American Population Growth

Generally speaking, emigration serves as a safety valve for less-developed countries suffering the acute pressures of rapid population growth. The exception to the rule is found in the so-called "brain drain," the flight of highly trained technical and scientific personnel from poor countries to wealthier ones. Nearly half of the physicians licensed in the United States in a recent year were graduates of foreign medical schools. Nearly three-fourths of these physicians (70 per cent) came from the less-developed countries.[10]

Emigration also has measurable effects on the host country. The U.S. Commission on Population Growth and the American Future noted in 1972 that between 1960 and 1970, legal immigration accounted for 16 per cent of the U.S. annual population growth; in 1971, it was responsible for 18 per cent; and by 1972, it had jumped to 23 per cent. This meant that roughly one new American out of four that year was an immigrant. Census Bureau estimates indicated that the current annual rate of legal immigration—approximately 400,000 persons per year—will add 13.4 million to the U.S. population by the year 2000, and 48.8 million by 2050. The Census Bureau has no projections for the impact of illegal immigration, but Zero Population Growth Inc. (ZPG), a nationwide lobby group dedicated to reducing U.S. population growth, calculates that illegal immigration will add 28 million people to the U.S. population by the year 2000, 59 million by 2025 and 80 million by 2050.[11] Zero Population Growth advocates restricting legal immigration to 150,000 persons a year.

The contribution of immigration to population growth does not lie solely in the number of people who enter the country. Demographers note that immigration tends to stimulate birth rates in receiving countries, particularly when immigrants come from high-fertility areas.[12] The influx of immigrants also can alter the age and sex composition of the population, which would influence the demand for social services and the growth of the labor force. Various studies have found that illegal aliens tend to be younger than the average American worker. The illegal group also apparently contains an imbalance of males over females.[13]

---

[10] See "The New Immigration," *E.R.R.*, 1974 Vol. II, pp. 929-930.

[11] *"Illegal Immigration,"* Fact Sheet issued by Zero Population Growth, July 1976.

[12] Harry W. Henderson and Leon F. Bouvier, "International Migration: An Overview," unpublished manuscript prepared for the Population Reference Bureau, Washington, D.C.

[13] See North and Houston, *op. cit.;* Julian Samora, *Los Mojados: The Wetback Story* (1971); and Immigration and Naturalization Service Annual Reports.

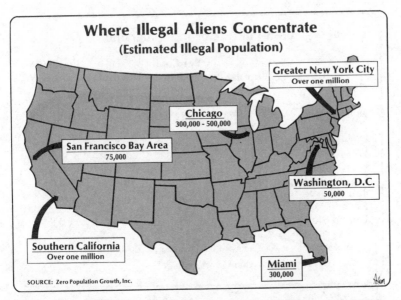

Where Illegal Aliens Concentrate
(Estimated Illegal Population)

Greater New York City
Over one million

Chicago
300,000 - 500,000

San Francisco Bay Area
75,000

Washington, D.C.
50,000

Southern California
Over one million

Miami
300,000

SOURCE: Zero Population Growth, Inc.

Illegal immigration also affects the distribution of the U.S. population. It is no longer true that persons who illegally cross the border from Mexico stay clustered in the American Southwest. They may now be found in most of the nation's major cities, from Boston to San Francisco *(see map)*.

Origin and Characteristics of Illegal Aliens

Migration results, in the words of demographers, from "push-pull" factors. Emigrants may be "pushed" out of their homelands by depressed economic conditions, unemployment, overcrowding and famines. They may be "pulled" to another country by the availability of jobs, higher living standards, better social facilities, and even a more pleasant climate

It is clear from a number of studies that the push-pull factors are operative in attracting illegal immigrants to the United States. In the case of Mexico, for example, the push stems from a high rate of population growth—3.5 per cent a year—and high unemployment rates, particularly in rural areas. The Mexican labor force, 16 million in 1970 is expected to rise to 28 million by 1985 and to 40 million in the mid-1990s. Not surprisingly, nearly 89 per cent of illegal Mexican aliens surveyed in the Labor Department study reported that they had come to the United States in search of work. To a lesser extent this was true of others from the Western Hemisphere; more than 60 per cent came for jobs. A majority of those deported indicated that they intended to return to the United States as soon as possible to find another job or, in a few cases, to return to a job that was being held open for them.

By far the greatest number of illegal persons in this country are Mexican nationals. Many are smuggled in by professional

Push-Pull Factor in Immigration

Country	Population Under 18	Per Capita Gross Product	Unemploy-ment Rate	Population Growth Rate*
Mexico	46%	US$1,000	10-14%	3.5%
Colombia	46	510	12-16	3.2
Canada	29	6,080	7	1.3
El Salvador	46	390	20-30	3.2
Guatemala	44	570	—	2.8
Dominican Repub.	48	590	15-20	3.0
Jamaica	46	1,140	—	1.9
Ecuador	47	460	—	3.2
United States	27	6,640	7.9	0.8

* Crude growth rate, not adjusted for emigration to the United States.

SOURCE: Zero Population Growth Inc.

rings at prices ranging up to $3,000. *The Washington Post* recently reported that 27 illegal aliens were smuggled across the border in California, jammed into a small van and were driven across the country in a day and night journey to Washington.[14] Some smuggling rings are so highly organized that prospective migrants frequently make only a small down payment before leaving home; they are driven to prearranged jobs and the smuggling fee is deducted from their wages.

The second largest category of illegal aliens is composed of visitors who enter the United States on visas permitting a limited stay and fail to leave on the assigned date of departure. The Immigration Service has said that up to 10 per cent of the 5.1 million tourists who visit the United States each year stay to find work. Some of them manage to become legal residents by entering into bona fide or sham marriages with U.S. citizens.

Although the Mexican border is the chief crossing point for illegal aliens, INS officials report increasing problems along the Canadian border, particularly in upper New York State and northern New England, and in Puerto Rico and the U.S. Virgin Islands. The Immigration Service has recently stepped up surveillance in these areas. Surveillance in the Caribbean is complicated by the fact that Virgin Islanders and Puerto Ricans are U.S. citizens, and INS inspectors may not detain a person without substantial grounds for suspecting that he or she is an illegal alien.

Although there are exceptions, most illegal immigrants are unskilled and lack education. Although a decreasing number

---

[14] *The Washington Post*, Nov. 20, 1976.

take jobs in agriculture, the employment they do find is usually menial and low paid. In this country, they become part of a hidden subculture. "They tend to group among themselves and to have few contacts with outsiders. There is a fairly well established communication network. First generation illegals tend to avoid any contacts with authority and generally live in fear of being caught."[15] In most cases, even this mode of existence is preferable to the life they left behind.

Approaches to Immigration Problems

ILLEGAL IMMIGRATION is not unique to the United States. It is a world-wide problem afflicting virtually all industrialized countries, and many less-developed countries as well. Wherever there are significant differences between countries in resources, employment, income and population growth, pressures for movement across national borders may be expected to develop. The United States is a powerful magnet to millions of impoverished Mexicans because of its employment opportunities and because the border makes migration relatively easy. However, the problem extends beyond the special U.S.-Mexican circumstances.

In this hemisphere, the exodus of 250,000 to 300,000 landless peasants from overcrowded El Salvador into Honduras was partly to blame for a brief but bloody war between the two countries in 1969.[16] The presence of up to one million illegal Colombians in the frontier states of Venezuela is a source of continuing tension between those two countries. Argentina has about 1,500,000 immigrants, mostly from Paraguay, Bolivia and Chile. Argentine authorities say 80 to 90 per cent of them are "undocumented."[17]

In Europe, the West German government estimates that between 250,000 and 500,000 illegal workers have been smuggled into the country despite a state-run program to sponsor the importation of legal workers. France reported in 1968 that 83 per cent of all aliens in that country were there illegally. Subsequently, the French government launched a program to "regularize" the status of illegal workers. France reported in

---

[15] National Council on Employment Policy, *op. cit.,* p. 17.

[16] "Population Imbalance Underlies El Salvador-Honduras Conflict," The Latin American Service, Washington, D.C., August 4, 1969.

[17] Charles B. Keeley and S. M. Tomasi, "The Disposable Worker: Historical and Comparative Perspectives on Clandestine Migration," paper presented at the Annual Meeting of the Population Association of America, Montreal, April 30, 1976, p. 27.

early 1974 that 38,500 illegals, mostly Tunisians and Moroccans, had accepted the government offer.[18] Other countries reporting large numbers of illegal aliens include South Africa, Australia, England, Canada, Japan and Hong Kong.

Illegal immigration is not a new problem in the United States. In the 1930s and again in the 1950s, public concern over the problem led the government to organize wholesale deportation programs. During both periods, bad economic conditions sharply reduced the demand for labor and illegal aliens were in open competition with U.S. citizens and legal resident aliens for scarce openings in the employment market.[19]

Patchwork Evolution of U.S. Immigration Laws

According to the National Council on Employment Policy, a private research organization in Washington, "Our nation's immigration policy is a patchwork of laws and approaches rather than a rational system."[20] Until the 1880s, the United States had no immigration policy at all. The nation was expanding, the frontier needed people, and the doors were open to all. In 1884, a decision was made to exclude the Chinese, largely because of their depressing effect on the labor market. Subsequently, the Japanese were barred, along with other categories of "undesirable" aliens such as paupers, lunatics and anarchists.

During World War I, Congress passed over President Wilson's veto the first law seriously limiting overall immigration. It mandated, among other requirements, a literacy test for prospective immigrants. During the postwar "Red Scare," Congress approved an "emergency" quota system limiting annual immigration from all countries outside the Western Hemisphere to 357,000. New temporary quotas were adopted in 1924, cutting the flow of immigrants from the Eastern Hemisphere to 164,000 a year. A permanent quota system based on national origins and favoring northern Europeans was instituted in 1929. It limited immigration from the Eastern Hemisphere to 159,981 a year.[21]

The national origin system was unaffected by changes in immigration law made by the McCarran-Walter Act of 1952.[22] The national origin system finally was abolished by the Immigration

[18] *Ibid.*, p. 26. See also "Europe's Foreign Laborers," *E.R.R.*, 1975 Vol. II, pp. 543-560.

[19] Charles M. Keeley, "Beyond Law Enforcement: Some Implications of a Perspective about Illegal Alien Policy in the U.S.," remarks at a briefing sponsored by Zero Population Growth, Washington, D.C., June 23, 1975.

[20] National Council on Employment Policy, *op. cit.*, p. 13.

[21] See "Ethnic America," *E.R.R.*, 1971 Vol. I, p. 47.

[22] The McCarran-Walter Act, officially known as the Immigration and Nationality Act of 1952, retained the system of quotas based on national origin and added token quotas for Asian countries and for new nations coming into existence. To limit overall immigration, the act continued to prohibit the transfer of unused quotas from one country to another. The act was named for its authors, Sen. Pat McCarran (D Nev.) and Rep. Francis E. Walter (D Pa.).

Act of 1965, which set overall annual quotas of 170,000 immigrants from the Eastern Hemisphere and 120,000 from the Western Hemisphere. A limit of 20,000 persons per country was set for the Eastern Hemisphere, while Western Hemispheric immigration was on a first-come, first-served basis. The Eastern Hemisphere also was made subject to a preference system,[23] which emphasized reunification of families rather than the needs of the labor market, a policy that has been called "nepotism." One study noted:

> The immigration now in place excludes the very kind of person who is most likely to want to immigrate to the United States, the kind that flocked to our shores at the turn of the century: the young, self-selected male, with more ambition than training, and with no family ties to the nation. It is no wonder, then,...that most of the illegals [are] young, self-selected males, with more ambition than education, and in most cases without the kinds of relatives needed to secure a visa.[24]

Ambiguity and Confusion in American Policy

Although there is substantial agreement among Americans that illegal aliens constitute a disturbing factor in U.S. society, there is a lack of adequate information on the extent of the problem. Among the charges being made against current immigration policy is that it is essentially two policies, each of which works against the other. On the one hand there is a *de jure* policy of virtual exclusion of unskilled immigrants, and on the other hand a *de facto* policy which encourages the influx of large numbers of them, especially in prosperous times when labor is in tight supply.[26] Employers currently are under no legal restraints not to hire illegal aliens. Several attempts to impose criminal or civil penalties on employers who hire illegal workers have failed in Congress.

Foes of such measures contend that the proposed penalties are not strong enough to be a deterrent to employers. Others say that such laws will make it easier for employers to discriminate against ethnic and minority-group persons and place the burden of enforcement on employers rather than the Immigration Service.

---

[23] The preferences, in order of priority, are: (1) Unmarried, adult children of citizens; (2) Spouses, unmarried adult children of resident aliens, and their children; (3) Immigrants in the professions, their spouses and children; (4) Married children of citizens, their spouses and children; (5) Brothers and sisters of citizens, their spouses and children; (6) Skilled workers, their spouses and children; (7) Refugees, their spouses and children. If quotas are not filled by the seven preference categories, an eighth non-preference category is included in the law. In addition, certain immigrants, such as the parents of U.S. citizens, are admitted without quota.

[24] North and Houston, *op. cit.*, p. 8.

[25] See Vernon M. Briggs Jr., "Illegal Immigration and the American Labor Force: The Use of (Soft) Data for Analysis," *American Behavioral Scientist*, Jan.-Feb., 1976, p. 352.

[26] See Keeley, *op. cit.*, p. 3, and National Council on Economic Policy, *op. cit.*, pp. 26-27.

The Immigration Service contends that Congress has been slow to increase the agency's budget to help it cope with the influx of illegal aliens. Commissioner Chapman has said, "With our limited manpower of less than 2,900 enforcement personnel to guard our nation's 6,000 miles of open-land border and seek out illegal aliens hidden among our population of over 210 million, the immigration laws of this country are unenforceable." Agreeing with Chapman, the General Accounting Office said: "INS does not have the problem under control. The increasing number of illegal aliens entering the country has reached severe proportions and far exceeds INS's ability to cope with the problem."[27]

The problem has many facets. A member of Congress, Rep. Henry Helstoski (D N.J.),[28] was indicted in June by a federal grand jury in Newark and awaits trial on charges that he extorted money from Argentine and Chilean aliens in exchange for sponsoring bills intended to benefit them. Illegal aliens have been found working in federal buildings, including the Immigration and Naturalization Service itself, and at work painting the Statue of Liberty. Perhaps strangest of all, each year on Washington's Birthday the U.S.-Mexican border is opened at the city of Laredo, Texas, to any and all comers for three days. Thousands of Mexicans pour across the border during the celebration, called "Paso Libre America" (Free Entry to America). According to Immigration officials, at least 10 per cent of the border crossers are making a one-way trip.[29]

Braceros and Green Card Commuters

There are several contradictions in current immigration law which many experts say breed disrespect for the law in the minds of American employers and potential immigrants. One is that it is possible for illegal aliens to adjust their status to that of legal immigrant. In some cases, illegal entrants apply for immigrant status in their own countries and then come to the United States to work while they await favorable action on their applications. In other cases, an illegal immigrant automatically receives permanent resident status by marrying a citizen or permanent resident. He or she also may qualify for permanent residence by acquiring a needed skill. In any event, the illegal immigrant runs little punitive risk; the worst that can happen is for him to be deported—to try again another day.

A fundamental assumption of U.S. immigration policy over the past century or more has been that an immigrant admitted

---

[27] Comptroller General of the United States, *"Immigration—Need to Reassess Policy,"* General Accounting Office, October 19, 1976.

[28] Helstoski was defeated for re-election, Nov. 2, 1976.

[29] *Los Angeles Times,* Feb. 22, 1976.

Deportable Aliens in the United States

Country	Fiscal Year 1975	Fiscal Year 1974	Percent- age Change
Mexico	680,392	709,959	− 4.2
Cuba	416	1,130	−63.2
Canada	9,048	9,362	− 3.4
Dominican Republic	3,233	3,601	−10.2
West Indies	7,094	5,512	+28.7
Other Western Hemispheric Countries	26,270	24,705	+ 6.3
China	4,213	4,204	+ 1.4
Philippines	3,164	2,804	+12.8
Greece	5,300	4,619	+14.7
Italy	1,941	1,570	+23.6
United Kingdom	2,664	2,334	+14.1
All Others	22,815	18,345	+24.4
Totals	766,600	788,145	− 2.7

SOURCE: *1975 Annual Report,* Immigration and Naturalization Service

to this country acquires most of the rights of a citizen. Until fairly recently, there has been no allowance for temporary workers who are neither permanent residents nor prospective citizens. This is not so in other nations. For example, there are some six-million so-called "guest workers" in the European Common Market countries.

The United States' primary experience with temporary workers was the Bracero Program, initiated during World War II to alleviate a temporary shortage of farm workers. Millions of Mexicans were admitted under temporary labor contracts. While an effort was made to assure decent working conditions and fair wages, the Braceros were, in effect, at the mercy of their employers. They were not permitted to seek other work, and they could be sent back to Mexico at the request of the employer. Controversial from the start, the program was ended in 1964.

Limited contract-worker programs, similar to the Bracero Program, still exist. West Indian seasonal farm workers are imported into Florida on so-called H-visas. In 1975, approximately 8,500 Jamaicans and "small islanders" (from the British West Indies) worked the Florida cane fields under contract with sugar cane producers. The U.S. Virgin Islands permitted entry of a number of "temporary" workers from the British West Indies in the mid-1950s. Many stayed on, worked their way up the economic ladder and, in time, became permanent residents.

Serious policy questions were raised when the Virgin Islands attempted to return these workers to their home islands during a recent period of recession and high unemployment.

Still another point of contention in immigration law is the "Texas Proviso," passed by Congress and signed by President Truman in 1952. It specifically exempts employers from the law making it a crime to conceal or harbor illegal aliens, declaring that employment may not be construed as "harboring." Perhaps the most curious contradiction is the existence of a fairly large number of persons who live in Canada and Mexico, and commute daily to work across the border into the United States. The largest group consists of the so-called Green-card commuters, who have acquired permanent resident status in legal ways but choose to live in their home countries.[30] Under a legal fiction, the Immigration Service considers the nightly return of the Green-carders to their homes a temporary visit overseas.

"With our [Immigration Service's] limited manpower [for apprehension of illegal aliens]...the immigration laws of this country are unenforceable."

Leonard F. Chapman Jr.,
Commissioner of the Immigration
and Naturalization Service

The service has said that there are some 60,000 commuting workers, although other estimates run as high as 75,000. A second category of commuting workers consists of citizens of the United States who live in Mexico and Canada and commute to jobs in the United States. This practice is particularly common along the Texas-Mexico border. In addition, a handful of Mexican and Canadian residents cross the border each day with non-immigrant visas which permit them to work in the United States. Finally, there are several hundred thousand persons living in border areas who hold "shoppers cards" permitting them access to the United States, but not the right to work here.

---

[30] "Green-card" refers to INS document No. I-151, which all permanent residents must carry, and which used to be green.

The Green-card system has been open to extensive fraud and misuse. Many illegal aliens have crossed the border using documents that were forged, altered or not their own. Beginning in January, the Immigration Service will issue a new tamper-proof, machine-readable card bearing the alien's photo, fingerprint, signature and basic physical data. The Service hopes to institute such a system to cover non-immigrant aliens as well, but achievement of that aim appears to be far in the future.

Search for Realistic Solutions

A GALLUP POLL conducted in 1976 for the Immigration and Naturalization Service showed that 74 per cent of those surveyed thought that illegal immigration was a serious concern. But while most Americans agree that there is a problem, they observe illegal immigration from different points of view and varying interests.

On one side are the farmers and growers who traditionally employ immigrants, both legal and illegal, in seasonal agricultural work. Impediments to the migratory flow would represent an economic threat. The growers are being joined by urban employers who find that employing illegal immigrants helps to slow down rising labor costs. For quite different reasons, support for illegal immigrants also comes from various religious groups, such as the National Catholic Conference which advocates an amnesty that would, in effect, legalize the status of all illegal aliens currently in this country. Civil rights groups, concerned with protecting immigrants and minority groups from discrimination and exploitation, have enlisted in the cause. Organized labor, while fearful of competition from low-wage illegal workers, generally supports measures to guarantee them fair wages and decent working conditions.

Opposing liberalized immigration policies is an equally strange coalition of interest groups. The Immigration Service is dedicated to enforcing the immigration laws now on the books and seeks additional support and funding for the apprehension of illegal aliens. Population groups, such as Zero Population Growth, seek stricter immigration controls in the interest of slowing the nation's rate of population growth. Environmentalists are concerned with the increasing strain on resources and the environment posed by a growing population and rising levels of affluence. Social-policy organizations oppose liberalizing immigration laws because of the impact on unemployment rates.

Caught in the middle and highly ambivalent about the problem are American minority groups—especially the Spanish-speaking—who are themselves immigrants or descendents of immigrants. For Chicanos, Puerto Ricans, Cubans and other Latin Americans there is a natural empathy with the newly arrived. At the same time, they are keenly aware that illegal aliens pose a threat to their jobs and their access to social services. Cesar Chavez, the Mexican-American leader of the United Farm Workers, has complained about the use of Mexican strikebreakers against his efforts to organize farm workers in the Southwest. But under pressure from urban Mexican-American leaders, Chavez has urged that Mexicans be allowed to settle in the United States, to bring their families and become citizens.

The fear of racism in American attitudes and enforcement of immigration law is implicit in. the views of many minority groups. "Illegal alien is an invidious code for Spanish-speaking," according to Rep. Herman Badillo (D N.Y.), the first Puerto Rican to hold a voting seat in the House of Representatives. A Chinese-American states: "Racism is a consistent underlying dimension of our immigration policies.... From an immigrant group perspective, there are dangers in making employers liable for hiring aliens. If the Oriental experience is indicative, employers are likely to overreact, adopting discriminatory practices which affect many legal immigrants and which force foreign minorities into the worst jobs."[31]

Considerations for American Foreign Relations

According to INS Commissioner Chapman, nearly 10 per cent of the Mexican people are now living in the United States. Chapman also reported that a State Department survey showed that 40 per cent of the Haitians interviewed wanted to migrate to the United States.[32] These figures point up the magnitude of the foreign policy problem posed by illegal immigration.

International migration can be a disruptive factor in relations between nations, as was the case of the 1969 war between El Salvador and Honduras. U.S. policy makers tend to consider the negative impact of illegal immigration on the American economy. There also is an impact, both negative and positive, on the sending countries. Large-scale, permanent emigration deprives sending countries of some of their most productive workers. If the emigrants are skilled, or even semi-skilled, labor shortages can arise in critical areas of the economy.

---

[31] Betty Lee Sung, quoted in "Illegal Aliens: An Assessment of the Issues," National Council on Employment Policy, p. 16.

[32] Chapman, *op. cit.*, p. 7.

Sources of Legal Immigration From Latin America

Country	1965	1975
Mexico	37,969	62,205
Cuba	19,760	25,955
Dominican Republic	9,504	14,066
Colombia	10,885	6,434
Ecuador	4,392	4,727
El Salvador	1,768	2,416
Other	22,629	14,218
Totals	106,907	130,021

SOURCE: Immigration and Naturalization Service

While outmigration may provide temporary relief to a government plagued by rapid population growth and high unemployment, it may also lull the government into postponing needed improvements in economic and social conditions. While Mexico, for example, can conceivably afford to lose 5 or even 10 per cent of its population each year, it cannot continue to put off measures to restrict population growth, redistribute land and restructure the labor market. Furthermore, it is inconceivable that any country—even one so desperately poor as Haiti—could afford to lose 40 per cent of its population in so short a time.

U.S. officials also must consider the global impact of a massive repatriation and deportation program, should the United States choose to initiate one. An abrupt reversal of the migratory flow could have disastrous effects on the sending countries. For example, Puerto Rico's industrial development in the 1950s and 1960s was aided and sustained by large-scale emigration from the island to the U.S. mainland.[33] In the 1970s, the migratory flow turned around; more Puerto Ricans returned to the island than left it. Puerto Rico fell into a recession far deeper than that which afflicted the United States. A similar reversal of migratory patterns in Mexico, resulting in the sudden return of three to five million expatriates, could have disastrous effects on Mexico's economic and political stability. Because of its proximity to Mexico, the United States can ill-afford to be indifferent to such a possibility.

Short Term Immigration Policy Alternatives

Recommendations for dealing with illegal immigration problems generally focus on law enforcement and compliance.

---

[33] See "Puerto Rico After Bootstrap," *E.R.R.*, 1971 Vol. I, p. 389.

There is a consensus, particularly among government officials, that steps must be taken to make illegal border crossing more difficult, to tighten safeguards against visa abuse, and to prevent the repeated return to this country of violators of the immigration laws.

In addition, some policy makers would like to remove the incentives that prompt employers to hire illegal workers. They advocate passage of an "Employer Sanctions" bill to set stiff penalties for knowingly hiring an illegal alien. Unclear as yet is how the government would establish that a violator had knowledge of illegal alien status, and how the system could be protected against racism and discrimination. Despite the inherent difficulties, a few states have passed such laws, and the Supreme Court has affirmed state jurisdiction in such matters in the absence of federal legislation. Coupled with an Employer Sanctions bill would be a general amnesty for illegals in this country, permitting them to assume permanent resident status.

Some persons also advocate adoption of a nationwide identification system for citizens and residents of the United States. Proponents of such a measure have suggested that the Social Security system be adapted to provide a universal identification card. Many foreign countries issue citizen identification cards, which must be produced on demand by a law enforcement official. The proposal is bitterly resisted by civil libertarians who say the invasion of privacy and the threat of regimentation is too great a price to pay for reduced illegal immigration.

Another plan for eliminating incentives to hire illegal aliens calls for institution of a temporary worker program, permitting aliens to enter the country for specific jobs but not to apply for permanent resident status or citizenship. However, the idea of a two-tier classification of people is repugnant to many Americans.

Need for Reassessment of Illegal Immigration

Most policymakers in this field recommend increased funding of federal activities to stem illegal immigration. Specific recommendations include: (1) additional staff and money for the Immigration Service to step up border surveillance and improve follow-up checks on visitors to this country; (2) stiffer penalties for visa abusers; (3) mandatory deportation for illegals apprehended by the Immigration Service (in many cases illegals are released in return for a promise to leave the country in a specified period of time); and (4) the creation of employers "strike forces," to monitor compliance not only with immigration law, but with tax and labor standards as well.

Many of these recommendations would correct obvious deficiencies in current federal efforts to cope with the flood of illegal immigrants. They leave untouched, however, the underlying causes of illegal immigration. A leading authority, Professor Charles B. Keeley of Fordham University, has said: "I would not expect control and law enforcement to end illegal immigration."[34]

Keeley and others would prefer to attack the push-pull factors that create the international migratory flow. The real cause of illegal immigration, they say, is the vast economic disparity between the industrialized countries and their poorer neighbors. So long as these disparities exist, the rich countries will hold an irresistible attraction for the disadvantaged people of the poor countries. Population and labor-force problems in less-developed countries cannot be controlled by law enforcement, however vigorously applied. A one-sided reliance on law enforcement moves against powerful economic and social currents that are transnational in character. The victims of such a policy are America's domestic poor, who must compete for substandard wages with the illegal immigrants, and the illegal aliens who are blamed for reacting to economic problems beyond their control.

To a certain extent, the United States can reduce the push factor by upgrading low-level jobs, enforcing labor standards and effectively restricting jobs to U.S. citizens and legal aliens with work authorizations. Even the least alluring jobs can be made attractive to unemployed Americans if the pay is sufficient and the working conditions tolerable. But in the end, the pull factor is the predominant one. Economic development of the poorer countries, particularly Mexico, may be the only effective policy.

---

[34] Keeley, *op. cit.*, p. 5.

Selected Bibliography

Books

Galarza, Ernesto, *Merchants of Labor: The Mexican Bracero Story,* McNally & Loflin, 1964.

McWilliams, Carey, *North from Mexico,* Greenwood Press, 1968.

Samora, Julian, *Los Mojados: The Wetback Story,* University of Notre Dame, 1971.

Articles

"A Population Policy for the United States," Zero Population Growth *National Reporter,* November 1976.

Briggs, Vernon M. Jr., "Illegal Immigration and the American Labor Market," *American Behaviorial Scientist,* January-February 1976.

Gottron, Martha V., "Illegal Alien Curbs: House Action Stalled," *Congressional Quarterly Weekly Report,* March 17, 1976.

Stoddard, Ellwyn R., "Illegal Mexican Labor in the Borderlands: Institutionalized Support of an Unlawful Practice," *Pacific Sociological Review,* April-July 1976.

Reports and Studies

Comptroller General of the U.S., "Immigration—Need to Reassess U.S. Policy," General Accounting Office, Oct. 19, 1976.

Editorial Research Reports, "The New Immigration," 1974 Vol. II, p. 927; "Ethnic America," 1971 Vol. I, p. 47; "Spanish-Americans: The New Militants," 1970 Vol. II, p. 707.

Henderson, Harry W. and Leon F. Bouvier, "International Migration—An Overview," unpublished manuscript prepared for Population Reference Bureau, Inc. (undated).

Karkashian, John E., "The Illegal Alien," case study prepared for 18th session, Senior Seminar in Foreign Policy, Department of State, 1976.

Keeley, Charles B. and S. M. Tomasi, "The Disposable Worker: Historical and Comparative Perspectives on Clandestine Migration," paper presented at the annual meeting of the Population Association of America, session on Clandestine Migration, Montreal, April 30, 1976.

Lesko Associates, "Basic Data and Guidelines Required to Implement a Major Illegal Alien Study during Fiscal Year 1976," Immigration and Naturalization Service, Oct. 15, 1976.

National Council on Employment Policy, "Illegal Aliens: An Assessment of the Issues," October 1976.

North, David S. and Marion F. Houston, "The Characteristics and Role of Aliens in the U.S. Labor Market: An Exploratory Study," Linton & Co., prepared for the U.S. Department of Labor, March 1976.

U.S. Congress, "Illegal Aliens," Hearings before the Subcommittee on Immigration, Citizenship, and International Law of the Committee on the Judiciary, Feb. 4, 26; March 5, 12, 13, and 19, 1975.

U.S. Immigration and Naturalization Service, Annual Reports.

Zero Population Growth, Inc., "Illegal Immigration," Fact Sheet, July 1976.

R EVERSE DISCRIMINATION

by

Sandra Stencel

**Aug. 6
1976**

Editor's Note: Since this Report was originally published, the Supreme Court has agreed to hear—and expects to decide in the current term—the Bakke case involving alleged reverse discrimination. It has often been called the most important civil rights case to come before the court since the landmark 1954 ruling in *Brown v. Board of Education* that struck down "separate but equal" segregation laws.

Regents of the University of California v. Allan Bakke involves a suit filed by Bakke, who is white, charging that the University of California at Davis wrongly rejected his application to its medical school while admitting minority-group applicants who scored lower on adminission tests than he did. The California Supreme Court agreed that he had been deprived of equal protection under the law, in violation of the Constitution. Thereupon, the board of regents appealed to the U.S. Supreme Court, which accepted the case and heard arguments last fall.

REVERSE DISCRIMINATION

I N TEXAS, two white employees of a Houston trucking firm were fired in 1970 after being charged with stealing 60 one-gallon cans of antifreeze from a customer's shipment. A black worker charged with the same offense was kept on.

In Virginia, 328 men and 57 women applied for two full-time positions in the sociology and anthropology department of Virginia Commonwealth University. No men were interviewed for the jobs; two women were hired.

In Chicago, on Jan. 5, 1976, U.S. District Court Judge Prentice H. Marshall gave the city 90 days to hire 400 new police officers. Of these, 200 were to be black and Spanish-named men and 66 were to be women. The judge also imposed a similar quota on future hiring.

In California, a white student was denied admission to the law school at the University of California's Davis campus in 1975 even though he had better grades and test scores than 74 other applicants admitted under a special minority admissions program.

These incidents and others like them have sparked an increasingly bitter debate over what has come to be known as "reverse discrimination"—giving preferential treatment to women, blacks and persons from other minority groups in such areas as employment and college admissions. The policy is defended as fair and necessary to compensate for past discrimination. It is criticized as "robbing Peter to pay Paul." The critics say that all persons should be judged solely on their personal qualifications.

The furor stems from the government's decade-old policy of requiring educators and employers to take "affirmative action" to prevent racial or sexual discrimination. To make up for alleged past discriminatory hiring practices, the government forced businesses and organizations holding federal contracts to set up goals and timetables for hiring minorities and women. Many employers complain that they are trapped between the government's demands to increase opportunities for women and minorities on the one hand, and, on the other, charges by white males that affirmative action constitutes reverse discrimination.

Growing numbers of white males, charging that they are victims of reverse discrimination, are going to court seeking redress. "The suits present a thorny problem for the courts," said *U.S. News & World Report.* "On the one hand, the preferences being attacked have a legally sanctioned goal—the correction or prevention of racial or sexual bias. But those not covered by such preferences charge it is just as illegal to discriminate against whites and males as against minorities and women."[1]

A recent ruling by the U.S. Supreme Court could result in a significant increase in lawsuits charging reverse discrimination. The Court ruled on June 25, 1976, that the Civil Rights Acts of 1866 and 1964 protect white people as well as blacks against racial discrimination. The ruling was the result of a suit filed by the two white employees of the Houston trucking firm who were fired for stealing company cargo although a black man who participated in the theft was not. With the help of the U.S. Equal Employment Opportunity Commission, the two men sued the company and their union on discrimination charges. The case was dismissed in lower federal court, which held that only minority group members could bring such charges under these laws. But on appeal the Supreme Court ruled the suit valid and held that the two civil rights laws ban discrimination against whites "upon the same standards as would be applicable were they Negroes."

The full meaning of the court's decision is not yet clear. To some observers it appeared to cast doubt on hiring and promotion quotas that favor blacks and women over white males. However, Justice Thurgood Marshall, author of the majority opinion, said the Court was not considering the legality of affirmative action programs.

Suits by White Males Charging Discrimination

The Supreme Court earlier had sidestepped a decision on reverse discrimination in the highly publicized DeFunis case *(see p. 156).* The plaintiff, Marco DeFunis, charged that he had been turned down by the University of Washington Law School while minority applicants with lower grades and test scores were admitted. When the Court in 1974 refused to decide the case on its merits, four justices dissented. One of the four, William J. Brennan, said: "Few constitutional questions in recent years have stirred as much debate, and they will not disappear. They must inevitably return to the federal courts and ultimately again to this court."

Several cases alleging reverse discrimination are expected to come before the Supreme Court in the near future. A definitive

---

[1] " 'Reverse Discrimination'—Has It Gone Too Far?" *U.S. News & World Report,* March 29, 1976, p. 26.

AT&T Cases

The legal complexities involved in reverse discrimination are perhaps best illustrated by a recent court ruling against American Telephone and Telegraph Co. In 1973, after more than two years of litigation, AT&T agreed to hire and promote thousands of women and minority group members. Following the guidelines laid out in their court-approved affirmative action plan, AT&T promoted a woman service representative over a male employee who had more experience and seniority. The man sued, contending that he was a victim of sex discrimination.

On June 9, 1976, U.S. District Court Judge Gerhard Gesell of Washington, D.C., ordered AT&T to pay the man an undetermined sum in damages. Although Judge Gesell held that the company had acted correctly in promoting the woman, he went on to say that the impact of its past discriminatory policies should fall on the company, not on "an innocent employee who had earned promotion." On the other hand, Gesell ruled that the man was entitled only to damages. To award him the promotion he was denied "might well perpetuate and prolong the effects of the discrimination [the 1973 agreement] was designed to eliminate."

If Judge Gesell's opinion is upheld by the higher courts, employers will face yet another expensive cost in complying with court orders to correct past discriminatory employment practices.

ruling would provide welcome guidance to the lower courts which have handed down contradictory rulings. In several recent cases the courts have ruled in favor of men who charged that employers were giving preferential treatment to women and minorities. For example, on June 9, U.S. District Court Judge Gerhard Gesell of Washington, D.C., ordered the American Telephone & Telegraph Co. to pay damages to a male employee passed over for promotion in favor of a less-experienced woman *(see box above)*.

Another federal judge in the District of Columbia, Oliver Gasch, ruled on July 28 that Georgetown University's policy of setting aside 60 per cent of its first-year law school scholarships for minority students constituted reverse discrimination and therefore violated the 1964 Civil Rights Act. The ruling came in a suit filed by a white student, J. Michael Flanagan, who claimed he was discriminated against because no more scholarships were available for white students by the time he had been admitted to the law school, although scholarship funds still were available for minority students.

In the case involving Virginia Commonwealth University, U.S. District Court Judge D. Dortch Warriner of Richmond ruled on May 28 that the school had acted illegally when it gave hiring preferences to women over equally qualified male applicants. The suit was filed by Dr. James Albert Cramer, a professor with temporary status in the school's sociology department and one of the 328 men to apply for full-time positions. Cramer contended that the university, in denying him a job because he was male, violated the Fourteenth Amendment's guarantee of equal protection under the law and the Civil Rights Act which bans discrimination on the basis of race, color, religion, sex or national origin. The university argued that under state and federal guidelines it was required to take affirmative action to hire women and minorities to "eliminate the effects of past discrimination" against them.

Judge Warriner held that under the equal-protection clause, "where sex is the sole factor upon which differential treatment is determined, there is no constitutional justification for treating the sexes differently." He said that even if the university was guilty of past discrimination, its preferential policies were unconstitutional because the civil rights law prohibits employment practices that "predicate hiring and promotion decisions on gender-based criteria."

In contrast, some other recent court rulings have upheld preferential treatment as a legal way of overcoming the effects of past discrimination. For example, the New York State Court of Appeals on April 8 held that the Brooklyn Downstate Medical Center had acted properly when it gave certain admissions preferences to minority applicants. The court said that reverse discrimination was constitutional "in proper circumstances." The test of constitutionality, the court held, should be "whether preferential treatment satisfies a substantial state interest.... It need be found that, on balance, the gain to be derived from the preferential policy outweighs its possible detrimental effects."

Case For and Against Preferential Treatment

Many of those who advocate preferential hiring and admissions policies deny that it amounts to reverse discrimination. "There is no such thing as reverse discrimination," said Herbert Hill, national labor director for the National Association for the Advancement of Colored People. "Those who complain of it are engaging in a deliberate attempt to perpetuate the racial status quo by drawing attention away from racial discrimination to make the remedy the issue. The real issue remains racial discrimination."[2]

Others, while acknowledging the dilemmas posed by preferential treatment, insist that such policies are necessary to wipe out the effects of past discrimination. "While there may be an element of unfairness in preferential treatment," said the authors

---

[2] Quoted in " 'Reverse Discrimination'—Has It Gone Too Far?" *U.S. News & World Report*, March 29, 1976, p. 29.

Preferential Treatment: Two Views

"Preferential remedies to end employment discrimination may be likened to starting one controlled forest fire in order to bring a raging one under control. At first the idea may seem illogical, but the remedial principle is sound."

—Professors Harry T. Edwards and Barry L. Zaretsky
Michigan Law Review

"There is no constitutional right for any race to be preferred."

—Supreme Court Justice William O. Douglas in
DeFunis v. Odegaard

"...[A] preference which aids minorities is perfectly consistent with the purpose of the Fourteenth Amendment."

—Brief submitted to Supreme Court in *De Funis v. Odegaard*

"Where individuals have overcome individual hardship, they should be favored, but what offends me deeply is the shorthand we use, which is race."

—Professor Alan Dershowitz of Harvard Law School quoted in *The New Republic*

"The reverse discrimination aspect of affirmative action is, in reality, the removal of that benefit which American society has so long bestowed, without question, upon its privileged classes."

—Shirley E. Stewart,
Cleveland State Law Review

the longstanding pervasive patterns of race and sex bias in this nation. The minor injustice that may result...is, on balance, outweighed by the fact that temporary preferential remedies appear to be the only way to effectively break the cycle of employment discrimination and open all levels of the job market to all qualified applicants."[3]

Affirmative action, it is pointed out, is not the first government program to prescribe differential treatment as a social policy. The Veterans Preference Act of 1944 stipulated that veterans should be given special consideration when seeking employment with the federal government. This statute granted persons extra points on competitive civil service examinations solely because they were veterans.

Economic statistics also provide an argument for the preferential treatment of minorities and women. According to the Census Bureau's latest findings, for 1974, black families had a median income of $7,808—half of the families earned more and half earned less. That was only 58 per cent of the white families' median income ($13,356), a drop of three percentage points since 1969.[4] There is a similar—and widening—gap between the earnings of men and women. The Department of Labor reported the median income of full-time women workers in 1975 was $6,975 while that of men was $12,152; women's earnings thus were only 57 per cent as high as men's, down from 64 per cent in 1955. *The Wall Street Journal* observed: "The average female college graduate earned less last year than the average male high-school dropout."[5]

Critics of affirmative action charge that the original purpose of that policy—the achievement of full and equal employment and educational opportunities—has been perverted. This theme dominates a controversial new book, *Affirmative Discrimination: Ethnic Inequality and Public Policy* (1975) by Harvard sociologist Nathan Glazer. He wrote: "In the early 1970s, affirmative action came to mean much more than advertising opportunities actively, seeking out those who might not know of them, and preparing those who might not yet be qualified. It came to mean the setting of statistical requirements based on race, color and national origin...." As a consequence of this shift in policy, Glazer said, "Those groups that are not considered eligible for special benefits become resentful."

[3] Harry T. Edwards and Barry L. Zaretsky, "Preferential Remedies for Employment Discrimination," *Michigan Law Review*, November 1975, p. 7. Edwards is a professor of law at the University of Michigan and Zaretsky is an assistant professor of law at Wayne State University.

[4] See U.S. Bureau of the Census, Current Population Reports, Special Studies, Series P-23 No. 54, "The Social and Economic Status of Black Population in the United States, 1974."

[5] *The Wall Street Journal*, July 6, 1976. See also U.S. Department of Labor, "1975 Handbook on Women Workers," and Lester C. Thurow's "The Economic Status of Minorities and Women," *Civil Rights Digest*, winter-spring 1976, pp. 3-9.

Glazer also raised the question of which groups should qualify for special treatment.

> The statistical basis for redress makes one great error: All "whites" are consigned to the same category, deserving of no special consideration. That is not the way "whites" see themselves, or indeed are, in social reality. Some may be "whites," pure and simple. But almost all have some specific ethnic or religious identification, which, to the individual involved, may mean a distinctive history of past—or perhaps some present—discrimination.

"Compensation for the past is a dangerous principle," Glazer went on to say. "It can be extended indefinitely and make for endless trouble."

Disputes Over Hiring and Admissions in Academia

The backlash against affirmative action and preferential treatment has been particularly strong in the academic community. "By using statistics to determine the presence of discrimination and ignoring differences in qualifications, the federal government is undermining the integrity and scholarly function of the university," Professor Allan C. Ornstein of Loyola University of Chicago has written.[6] Government intrusion into more and more aspects of university life was the theme of the 1974-1975 annual report issued recently by Harvard President Derek Bok.

> In a few short years [he said], universities have been encumbered with a formidable body of regulations, some of which seem unnecessary and most of which cause needless confusion, administrative expense and red tape. If this process continues, higher education will almost certainly lose some of the independence, the flexibility and the diversity that have helped it to flourish in the past.

Bok was particularly concerned about the mounting costs of complying with federal regulations.[7] It has been reported elsewhere, for example, that when Reed College in Portland, Ore., sought to hire some new faculty members recently, it was told by the Department of Health, Education and Welfare—which is responsible for administering affirmative action programs in educational institutions—to advertise nationally instead of going through normal academic channels. As a result, the small private college was flooded with some 6,000 applications. In addition, HEW demanded that Reed keep records on all the applicants not hired and make detailed reports on prime candidates who reached the finals, including their race, sex, qualifications, prior experience, and why Reed did not hire

---

[6] Allan C. Ornstein, "Quality, Not Quotas," *Society*, January-February 1976, p. 10.
[7] See "Future of Private Colleges," *E.R.R.*, 1976 Vol. I, pp. 305-322.

them.[8] The University of California at Berkeley has estimated that it will spend some $400,000 to implement an affirmative action plan.

Some educators charge that the government is forcing colleges to hire underqualified and unqualified persons merely because they are women or members of a minority group. Colleges that fail to comply face the loss of federal funds which can amount to millions of dollars. In 1971, for example, HEW froze $13-million in federal research contracts with Columbia University when the school failed to come up with an acceptable affirmative action plan. Educators often tell the story of the HEW representative who, when informed that there were no black teachers in the religion department of Brown University because none who applied met the requirements for ancient languages, replied: "Then end these old-fashioned programs that require irrelevant languages."[9]

HEW has shown some sensitivity to the special characteristics of academic employment. In December 1974 it reviewed the existing codes applying to affirmative action. This "memorandum to college and university presidents," signed by Peter E. Holmes, director of the department's Office of Civil Rights, stated that under existing law, colleges and universities could hire the "best qualified" person for a position. The memo concluded that the legal commitment to affirmative action merely required a school to show "good faith attempts" to recruit women and minorities.

What disturbs some eduators more than reverse discrimination are signs that preferential admissions to professional schools have brought in students who cannot do the work. Dr. Bernard D. Davis, a professor of bacterial physiology at Harvard Medical School, suggested recently that academic standards in the nation's medical schools have fallen in recent years because of the rise in the number of students with "substandard academic qualifications."

"It would be a rare person today," he wrote in *The New England Journal of Medicine*, "who would question the value of stretching the criteria for admission, and of trying to make up for earlier educational disadvantages...." But in their eagerness to help disadvantaged students, he charged, some medical schools are graduating students who may not be qualified to be doctors. He cited the example of one unidentified student who had been awarded a degree although he failed to pass a mandatory examination in five attempts. "It would be cruel," Dr. Davis wrote, "to admit students who have a very low probability of measuring up to reasonable standards. It is even crueler to abandon those

---

[8] See Ralph Kinney Bennett's "Colleges Under the Federal Gun," *Readers Digest*, May 1976, p. 126.

[9] The university later received an apology from HEW for the representative's remarks.

standards and allow the trusting patients to pay for our irresponsibility."[10]

The number of black students in American medical schools has increased greatly in recent years, from 783 in 1968 to 3,456 in 1976, in part because of special-admission efforts. There is also evidence of a higher failure rate among black students. At the University of Michigan Medical School, for example, the failure rate is 20 per cent for blacks and 4 per cent for whites. Recent medical school graduates of predominantly black Howard University, *The Washington Post* has reported, have failed their national board examinations—the final tests most medical school graduates take to become doctors—at a rate three and a half times above the national average.

Those who support preferential admissions to medical schools say that grades and test scores are not always a good indication of who will make good doctors. Said Dr. Alvin Poussaint, dean of student affairs at Harvard Medical School, "We need caring doctors, doctors with concerns and abilities not disclosed on the standards tests."[11]

Development of Affirmative Action

WHEN CONGRESS passed the Civil Rights Act in 1964, it was generally believed that discrimination took place primarily through conscious, overt actions against individuals. But it quickly became apparent that the processes of discrimination were much more subtle and complex than originally envisioned. It was discovered that normal, seemingly neutral policies such as seniority, aptitude and personnel tests, high school diploma requirements and college admission tests could perpetuate the effects of past discrimination. This led to the development of the affirmative action concept.

The need for affirmative action was spelled out by President Johnson in a commencement address at Howard University on June 4, 1965.

> Freedom is not enough [Johnson said]. You do not wipe out scars of centuries by saying "now you're free to go where you want and do as you desire." You do not take a person who for years has been hobbled by chains and liberate him, bringing him up to the

---

[10] Bernard D. Davis, "Academic Standards in Medical Schools," *The New England Journal of Medicine*, May 13, 1976. His article drew widespread criticism, including charges of racism, and he subsequently said it had been misrepresented in the press.

[11] Quoted in *The Washington Post*, June 1, 1976.

starting line of a race and then say "you're free to compete" and justly believe that you have been completely fair.

The following Sept. 24 Johnson issued Executive Order 11246 requiring federal contractors "to take affirmative action to ensure that applicants are employed, and that employees are treated during employment, without regard to their race, creed, color or national origin."[12] Every major contractor—one having more than 50 employees and a contract of $50,000 or more with the federal government—was required to submit a "written affirmative action compliance program" which would be monitored by the Department of Labor's Office of Federal Contract Compliance.

In January 1970, Secretary of Labor George P. Schulz issued guidelines for the affirmative action plans required by the executive order. The guidelines, which were revised in December 1971, stated that affirmative action was "results oriented." A contractor who was considered to have too few women or minority employees had to establish goals for each job classification, by sex and race, and timetables specifying the date when the situation would be corrected.

Philadelphia Plan Controversy Over Job Quotas

The Department of Labor had already—on June 29, 1969—announced a plan to increase minority employment in the construction trades in Philadelphia. The "Philadelphia Plan" set goals for the number of blacks and other minority workers to be hired on construction projects financed by federal funds. Secretary Schulz stressed that contractors who could not meet the hiring goals would not be penalized if they showed a "good faith effort" to fulfill them.

Controversy over the plan arose on Aug. 5 when Comptroller General Elmer B. Staats[13] issued a ruling that the Philadelphia Plan violated the 1964 Civil Rights Act by requiring racial hiring quotas. Staats dismissed the plan's distinction between a quota system and a goal system as "largely a matter of semantics." The purpose of either, he said, was to have contractors commit themselves to considering race or national origin in hiring new employees.

The Nixon administration continued to defend the plan. It pointed out that Congress had given the Attorney General, not the Comptroller General, authority to interpret the 1964 Civil Rights Act and that Attorney General John Mitchell had approved the Philadelphia Plan. It was incorrect, Mitchell said in a statement issued Sept. 22, 1969, to say that the 1964 act forbade

---

[12] Executive Order 11246 was amended in 1967 to apply to sexual discrimination.
[13] The Comptroller General of the United States works for Congress, not the executive branch.

employers to make race a factor in hiring employees. "The legal definition of discrimination is an evolving one," he said, "but it is now well recognized in judicial opinions that the obligation of non-discrimination, whether imposed by statute or by the Constitution, does not require, and, in some circumstances, may not permit obliviousness or indifference to the racial consequences of alternative courses of action...."

The Department of Labor put the Philadelphia Plan into effect the next day and soon afterward announced that similar plans would become effective in New York, Seattle, Boston, Los Angeles, San Francisco, St. Louis, Detroit, Pittsburgh and Chicago. The AFL-CIO and the building trades unions actively opposed such plans and lobbied for the inclusion of a provision in a 1970 appropriations bill to give the Comptroller General authority to block funds for any federal programs he considered to be illegal. Congress narrowly defeated this provision after President Nixon threatened to veto the appropriations bill if it was included. Critics of the Philadelphia Plan then turned to the courts, but in 1971 the plan was upheld in federal appeals court.[14]

Extension of Rules to Education; DeFunis Case

Educational institutions originally were not covered by the fair-employment section of the 1964 Civil Rights Act. This oversight was amended by the Equal Employment Act of 1972. "Discrimination against minorities and women in the field of education is as pervasive as discrimination in any other area of employment," said the House Committee on Education and Labor at the time. Similar views were expressed by the Senate Committee on Labor and Public Welfare: "As in other areas of employment, statistics for educational institutions indicate that minorities and women are precluded from the most prestigious and higher-paying positions, and are relegated to the more menial and lower-paying jobs."

According to Howard Glickstein, director of the Center for Civil Rights at the University of Notre Dame, the need for the inclusion of colleges and universities within the coverage of the Equal Employment Act was illustrated by the extent to which charges of discrimination have been filed with the EEOC. In 1973, he said, approximately one out of four EEOC charges involved higher education. "While a charge is not proof..., I believe that the large number of charges filed against educational institutions in the short time they have been covered by the act is indicative of a widespread and pervasive problem."[15]

---

[14] *Contractors Association of Eastern Pennsylvania* v. *Secretary of Labor*, 442 F 2d 159 (3d Cir. 1971).
[15] "Discrimination in Higher Education: A Debate on Faculty Employment," *Civil Rights Digest*, spring 1975, p. 12.

In addition to coping with charges of discrimination in employment, colleges and universities also were under heavy pressure to increase the number of women and minority students, particularly in graduate and professional schools.[16] To meet these demands most schools adopted preferential admissions programs, favoring minority group members.

Among the schools adopting a preferential admissions policy was the University of Washington. In 1971 its law school received 1,600 applications for 150 openings that September. Among the applicants rejected was Marco DeFunis, a white Phi Beta Kappa graduate of the university's undergraduate program. Among those admitted were 36 minority-group students whose grades and law school admission test scores were lower than those of DeFunis. The law school acknowedged that minority applicants had been judged separately. DeFunis sued, charging that he had been deprived of his constitutional right to equal protection under the law.

A trial court in Seattle agreed and ordered the school to enroll him. The university complied but appealed and the state supreme court, in 1973, ruled in favor of the school. DeFunis then appealed to the U.S. Supreme Court, and Justice William O. Douglas granted a stay that permitted him to remain in school pending a Supreme Court decision. But the Court, by a 5-4 vote on April 23, 1974, refused to decide the case—on the ground that the question was moot because DeFunis had been attending school and was expected to graduate within two months.

The Court's action was anti-climactic in a case which had produced substantial advance publicity. Some 64 organizations spoke up on the issue in 26 "friend of the court" briefs submitted to the Court. Among those submitting briefs supporting DeFunis were the Anti-Defamation League of B'nai B'rith, the Joint Civic Action Committee of Italian Americans, the Advocate Society (a Polish-American lawyers' association), the AFL-CIO, the National Association of Manufacturers and the U.S. Chamber of Commerce. Briefs defending the university were submitted by the former deans of the Yale and Harvard law schools, Louis Pollak and Erwin Griswold, the American Bar Association, the National Urban Coalition and a number of educational institutions, including the national associations of both law schools and medical schools.

Justice Douglas, one of the four dissenting justices, submitted a separate 29-page opinion in which he sharply criticized preferential admissions policies. Each application should be considered in a racially neutral way, Douglas emphasized: "A

---

[16] See "Blacks on Campus," *E.R.R.*, 1972 Vol. II, pp. 667-684.

DeFunis who is white is entitled to no advantage by reason of that fact; nor is he subject to any disability.... Whatever his race he had a constitutional right to have his application considered on its individual merits in a racially neutral manner."

But Douglas went on to say that schools should not have to judge applicants solely on the basis of their grades or test scores. A black applicant "who pulled himself out of the ghetto into a junior college...," Douglas wrote, "may thereby demonstrate a level of motivation, perseverance and ability that would lead a fair-minded admissions committee to conclude that he shows more promise for law study than the son of a rich alumnus who received better grades at Harvard."

Complaint Investigations and Leading Decisions

The Equal Employment Opportunity Commission was created by the 1964 Civil Rights Act to investigate employment discrimination complaints. In 1972, upon passage of the Equal Opportunity Act, the commission gained authority to bring civil suits directly against employers it found to be engaging in discriminatory practices. The EEOC's impact on American business has been characterized in a law journal in the following way:

> The period from 1964 to 1974 marked a major change not only in the composition of the national work force, but, perhaps more importantly, in the attitudes and personnel policies of those involved in the labor market. It was a decade in which employment expectations and opportunities of...blacks and women were expanded greatly. Employers and unions were forced to reconsider carefully their standards for hiring, promotion and membership.[17]

In most instances, change did not come easily or voluntarily. Most cases required court action. Some of the leading cases were these:

> Anaconda Aluminum Co. in 1971 was ordered to pay $190,000 in back wages and court costs to 276 women who alleged that the company maintained sex-segregated job classifications.

> Virginia Electric Power Co. in 1971 was ordered to pay $250,000 to compensate black workers for wages they would have earned if they had not been denied promotion by a discriminatory system. The company also was told that one-fourth of the new employees in union jobs should be non-white.

> Black employees of the Lorillard Corp. were awarded $500,000 in back pay in 1971 by a court that found contracts between the company and its union limited access of blacks to most jobs. The company and union were ordered to assure that blacks had equal opportunity for assignment and promotion in all jobs.

---

[17] "The Second Decade of Title VII: Refinement of the Remedies," *William and Mary Law Review*, spring 1975, p. 436.

The Household Finance Corp. was ordered in 1972 to pay more than $125,000 to women employees who charged that they were denied promotions because of their sex. HFC also agreed to train women and minority employees for better jobs.

The American Telephone & Telegraph Co., in one of the most important of all affirmative action settlements, agreed in January 1973 to open thousands of jobs to women and minority groups, and to pay $15-million in back wages for past discrimination *(see box, p. 45).*

The government won a significant victory in June 1974 when the Supreme Court ruled[18] that employers must pay men and women equal pay for what is essentially equal work. Under the ruling, Corning Glass Works of New York was ordered to pay approximately $500,000 in back pay to women who had been receiving a lower base salary for daytime work than men who did similar jobs at night. That same month the Bank of America reached an out-of-court settlement of a class-action suit filed on behalf of its women employees. Bank of America agreed (1) to pay an estimated $10-million in compensatory salary increases for its women employees, (2) to set up a $3.75-million trust fund for education and "self-development" programs for women employees, and (3) to increase the over-all proportion of women officers to 40 per cent by 1978, up from 18 per cent.

Merrill Lynch, Pierce, Fenner & Smith, the country's biggest securities firm, settled two separate but related bias suits on June 4, 1976, when it agreed to pay $1.9-million in back pay awards to women and minorities affected by alleged discriminatory hiring and promotion practices. Merrill Lynch also agreed to spend $1.3-million on a five-year affirmation action plan designed to recruit more women and minority employees.

Controversy Over Seniority Rights

E MPLOYMENT OPPORTUNITIES for women and minorities expanded rapidly between 1964 and 1973. By 1974, however, the situation had begun to change. The United States entered an economic recession and employers, both public and private, began to lay off workers, often using the long-accepted principle of "last hired, first-fired," whereby workers who lacked seniority were laid off first.

Fearing that this practice would erode the improvements in minority and female employment of the preceding years, civil rights advocates tried to outlaw the use of straight seniority

---

[18] *Corning Glass Works v. Brennan,* 427 U.S. 188.

systems, arguing that they perpetuated the effects of past discrimination. If women and minorities had not previously been discriminated against, it was said, they would have have an opportunity to build up more seniority. Minorities "are being penalized twice," said Herbert Hill of the NAACP, "once by not being hired, and now once they are hired, by being laid off first."[19] To remedy this situation and protect the job gains of women and minorities, some persons suggested a system of "artificial" or "retroactive" seniority dating from the time the employee originally was turned down for a job.[20]

Defenders of the "last in—first out" principle argued that it was a non-discriminatory way of dealing with job losses. Moreover, they said, granting seniority to someone who had not earned it amounted to reverse discrimination. The concept of "fictional" seniority is alien to American jurisprudence, said William Kilberg, a Department of Justice attorney.[21] Union officials said that seniority was too important to the daily lives of workers to be compromised. It affects not only layoff and rehiring policies, but promotions, vacations, transfers, overtime distribution, job assignments and even parking space. Often eligibility for pensions or profit sharing is related to length of service. Finally, pro-seniority forces pointed out, the 1964 Civil Rights Act upholds a "bona fide" seniority system.

Title VII, section 703 (h) states: "[I]t shall not be an unlawful employment practice for an employer to apply different standards of compensation, or different terms, conditions or privileges of employment pursuant to a bona fide seniority or merit system...provided that such differences are not the result of an intention to discriminate because of race, color, religion, sex or national origin..."

Title VII, section 703 (j) states: "Nothing contained in this title shall be interpreted to require any employer...to grant preferential treatment to any individual or to any group because of the race, color, religion, sex or national origin of such individual or group on account of an imbalance which may exist with respect to the total number or percentage of persons of any race, color, religion, sex or national origin employed by any employer..."

Supreme Court Ruling on Retroactive Seniority

Though the lower courts have split on the question of fictional seniority, the Supreme Court offered some clarification of the issue on March 24, 1976. It upheld the right to award seniority

---

[19] Quoted in "Last Hired, First Fired—Latest Recession Headache," *U.S. News & World Report,* April 7, 1975, p. 74.

[20] See Michael J. Hogan, "Artificial Seniority for Minorities As a Remedy for Past Bias vs. Seniority Rights of Nonminorities," *University of San Francisco Law Review,* fall 1974, pp. 344-359; Michael Joseph, "Retroactive Seniority—The Courts as Personnel Director," *Oklahoma Law Review,* winter 1976, pp. 215-223; and Donald R. Stacy, "Title VII Seniority Remedies in a Time of Economic Downturn" *Vanderbilt Law Review,* April 1975, pp. 487-520.

[21] Quoted by Bertrand B. Pogrebin, "Who Shall Work?" *Ms.,* December 1975, p. 71.

rights retroactively to persons who could prove they would have been hired earlier had they not suffered from illegal racial or sexual discrimination. Thus if a woman or a black had been rejected for a job in, say, 1970, and was finally hired in 1973, he or she today would be entitled to six years seniority instead of three.

The ruling came in a case brought by two black men—Harold Franks and Johnnie Lee—against Bowman Transportation Co. in Atlanta. Franks, a Bowman employee, had been denied a promotion because of his race. Lee was refused a driver's job on the same basis. Lower courts found clear evidence of illegal discrimination, and ordered the company to remedy its actions—but refused to go as far as to order the company to award Franks and Lee retroactive seniority.

The Supreme Court disagreed. Justice William J. Brennan, author of the majority opinion, asserted that if the person merely was awarded a job he should have had, he "will never obtain his rightful place in the hierarchy of seniority...He will perpetually remain subordinate to persons who, but for the illegal discrimination, would have been...his inferiors." Chief Justice Warren E. Burger, one of the three dissenting justices, said awards of retroactive seniority at the expense of other employees were rarely fair. "I cannot join in judicial approval of 'robbing Peter to pay Paul,'" he said. Burger suggested that victims of such discrimination be given a monetary award in lieu of the seniority grant. AFL-CIO Special Counsel Larry Gold said the ruling provided "full remedy to employees who have actually suffered from discrimination."[22] But at the same time labor spokesmen reiterated their opposition to any effort to undermine the basic principles of seniority systems.

Layoffs or Worksharing: A Search for Alternatives

The Franks case still leaves a number of questions unanswered. The ruling applies only to applicants who can prove they were victims of discrimination. What about persons who never bothered to apply for jobs because they were aware of a company's long history of discrimination? Are they entitled to fictional seniority also? Nor did the ruling resolve the "last hired—first fired" controversy. The Court currently is reviewing several petitions to hear cases seeking to abolish seniority systems that would affect a disproportionate number of minority and female workers in a layoff situation. Pro-seniority forces hope the Court follows the example of U.S. Appeals Court Judge Leonard I. Garth of Philadelphia who, in a case involving Jersey Central Power and Light Co., ruled in February 1975 that antidiscrimination goals cannot take precedence over workers'

---

[22] Quoted in *Time*, April 5, 1976, p. 65.

seniority rights in layoffs without a specific mandate from Congress.

Some companies are searching for alternatives to seniority-based layoffs. Some possibilities were discussed in February 1975 at a conference sponsored by the New York City Commission on Human Rights. One suggestion was to reduce the hours worked by all employees. This could be accomplished in several ways: shutting down the plant or office for a specified time per month, adopting a shorter workweek or workday, eliminating overtime, encouraging voluntary leaves of absence or early retirement. Employees also could be encouraged to accept voluntary wage cuts and deferral of raises, bonuses and cost-of-living increases. Furthermore, employers should determine if they could cut costs, other than wages, without interfering with plant operations or harming the position of minorities and women.

If layoffs were unavoidable, they could be made on a rotating basis so that each employee could work part of the time. This would spread the layoff burden among all employees rather than concentrating it among the newly hired. Another plan discussed at the New York conference was that of laying off newly hired women and minorities in the same proportion as the over-all layoff. For instance, if 10 per cent of the work force must be dismissed, just 10 per cent of the low-seniority women and minorities would lose their jobs. A few companies are even experimenting with "inverse seniority," which requires older employees who have accumulated high unemployment benefits—such as union-negotiated supplemental unemployment payments—to bear the brunt of layoffs.

Most people agree that the best solution to the layoff problem is full employment. But until that goal is reached the courts will have to determine where the rights of women and minorities end and where those of whites and males begin.

Selected Bibliography

Books

Glazer, Nathan, *Affirmative Discrimination: Ethnic Inequality and Public Policy,* Basic Books, 1975.

O'Neil, Robert M., *Discriminating Against Discrimination: Preferential Admissions and the DeFunis Case,* Indiana University Press, 1975.

Articles

Bennett, Ralph Kinney, "Colleges Under the Federal Gun," *Readers Digest,* May 1976.

Civil Rights Digest, spring 1975 issue.

Davis, Bernard D., "Academic Standards in Medical Schools," *The New England Journal of Medicine,* May 13, 1976.

Edwards, Harry T. and Barry L. Zaretsky, "Preferential Remedies for Employment Discrimination," *Michigan Law Review,* November 1975.

Egan, Richard, "Atonement Hiring," *The National Observer,* July 3, 1976.

Foster, J.W., "Race and Truth at Harvard," *The New Republic,* July 17, 1976.

Hechinger, Fred M., "Justice Douglas's Dissent in the DeFunis Case," *Saturday Review/World,* July 27, 1974.

Hook, Sidney and Miro Todorovich, "The Tyranny of Reverse Discrimination," *Change,* winter 1975-1976.

Joseph, Michael, "Retroactive Seniority—The Court as Personnel Director," *Oklahoma Law Review,* winter 1976.

Pogrebin, Bertrand B., "Who Shall Work?" *Ms.,* December 1975.

Society, January-February 1976 issue.

Stewart, Shirley E., "The Myth of Reverse Race Discrimination," *Cleveland State Law Review,* Vol. 23, 1974.

Thurow, Lester C., "The Economic Status of Minorities and Women," *Civil Rights Digest,* winter/spring 1976.

Virginia Law Review, October 1974 issue.

William and Mary Law Review, spring 1975 issue.

"Court Turning Against Reverse Discrimination," *U.S. News & World Report,* July 12, 1976.

"More Seniority for the Victims," *Time,* April 5, 1976.

"Racism in Reverse," *Newsweek,* March 11, 1974.

"Reverse Discrimination—Has It Gone Too Far?" *U.S. News & World Report,* March 29, 1976.

Reports and Studies

Editorial Research Reports, "Black Americans, 1963-1973," 1973 Vol. II, p. 623; "Blacks on Campus," 1972 Vol. II, p. 667; "Future of Private Colleges," 1976 Vol. I, p. 305.

U.S. Bureau of the Census, "The Social and Economic Status of the Black Population in the United States, 1974."

U.S. Department of Labor, "1975 Handbook on Women Workers."

U.S. Equal Employment Opportunity Commission, "Affirmative Action and Equal Employment: A Guidebook for Employers," January 1974.

PENSION PROBLEMS

by

Suzanne de Lesseps

**May 21
1 9 7 6**

Editor's Note: On page 178 it is mentioned that Alaskan state and New York City employees had filed notice with the Social Security Administration for withdrawal from participation in the federal Social Security System. During 1977, the Alaskan employees and all but three groups of New York City employees rescinded their withdrawal notices—so that they would remain covered by Social Security.

PENSION PROBLEMS

P ENSION PLANS for American workers that sprang up in
the prosperity of yesteryear are causing sobering second
thoughts in the mid-Seventies. The problem is funding and it extends to pension plans both in private industry and government
but especially to the latter. Many state and municipal
governments are becoming aware they have not set aside enough
funds to pay future pension costs. And in the federal government there are warnings that its pensions for civilian and
military employees are rising so fast they pose a financial
burden on the nation in the years ahead.

Critical scrutiny which only a few years ago focused on mismanagement and misuse of pension plans in private industry
has turned to the adequacy of financing in the government sector. Massachusetts, for example, has estimated it will need $4.7-
billion more than it has set aside for pension obligations. Los
Angeles puts its pension gap at $2.9-billion.[1] A recent report on
New York City's five pension plans concluded that their unfunded liabilities amounted to $6-billion. As of mid-1975, the future
deficit of the federal civil service retirement system was
calculated at $97.2-billion. While civil service pensions are par-
tially funded by employee contributions, the military retirement
system has no reserves at all and each year takes a larger chunk
out of the defense budget.

Sen. Thomas F. Eagleton (D Mo.) speaks of a "financial time
bomb ticking away in the inner reaches of government" and
Arthur F. Burns, chairman of the Federal Reserve Board, warns
of a "terrible day of reckoning" to come for local, state and
federal units of government in their pension funding. How soon
the underfunding reaches the critical stage at any given place
depends on how soon a large number of workers reach retirement age, according to Randall Weiss, an economist and pension
analyst at the University of Maryland.[2]

How has this situation been allowed to develop? State and
municipal officials have been under pressure from public-

---

[1] The total for one county and three city plans.

[2] Interview, April 30, 1976. Eagleton's comments were in a speech to the New York Society
of Security Analysts on Jan. 13, 1976. Burns' remarks were made to an informal gathering
with reporters. He was quoted by Richard L. Strout, *The Christian Science Monitor*, Dec. 24,
1975.

employee unions for years to increase pension benefits.[3] Many of the officials who supported the requests did not obtain tax raises to provide adequate funding. In addition, some states and cities have used pension contributions to meet more pressing needs. Dan McGill of the Wharton School of Finance and Commerce at the University of Pennsylvania, calls the underfunding of government-sponsored pension plans "one of the biggest scandals of our time."[4] In Illinois, Michigan, Pennsylvania and a number of other places, public employees have filed suit to force city officials to allocate more money to underfunded plans.

There are two basic ways of financing a pension plan. One system is known variously as *advance funding, actuarial funding* or *reserve funding.* Regardless of which name is applied, contributions are paid into a fund on a regular, systematic basis determined by projections of future needs. The other system, a *pay-as-you-go* plan, derives its funds from yearly appropriations of general revenues.

Pay-as-you-go financing was outlawed for private-employee pension plans by the federal Employee Retirement Income Security Act of 1974 to prevent companies that go out of business from leaving their retired employees without pension benefits. Public employees were not included under that law *(see p. 177).* In the past, state and municipal officials defended pay-as-you-go financing with the argument that taxes could be raised if more funding was necessary. New York City's flirtation with financial collapse has undermined that argument.

Political Conflicts in Management of Pensions

It is ironic that pension funds which contributed to New York City's problems have also aided in the city's rescue. When its finances reached a crisis stage in the fall of 1975, the initial bailout was with teacher retirement funds. Albert Shanker, president of the American Federation of Teachers, agreed after heated negotiations to invest $150-million of the funds in New York securities. He later charged that the pressure exerted on him was "intense, amounting to blackmail," but he added that the consequences of default would have been disastrous.[5]

The Shanker incident exemplifies one of the most frequent criticisms of public pension plans—it is that they are subject to political control and manipulation. Louis M. Kohlmeier, in a recent study done for the Twentieth Century Fund, outlined many of the conflicts of interest inherent in pension fund

---

[3] See "Public Employee Militancy," *E.R.R.*, 1975 Vol. II, pp. 685-704.
[4] Quoted in *U.S. News & World Report*, March 15, 1976.
[5] Quoted in *The New York Times*, Oct. 18, 1976.

Public Employee Retirement Systems, 1975*

	Number of Plans	Membership (in thousands)		
		Active	Inactive**	Total
State and local	6,076	10,268	2,374	12,642
Federal military	1	2,151	1,102	3,253
Federal civilian	64	2,883	1,570	4,453
Totals	6,141	15,302	5,046	20,348

* Preliminary figures compiled by the Pension Task Force of the House Subcommittee on Labor Standards
** Persons receiving benefits as well as former employees who have acquired a vested right to receive retirement benefits at a subsequent time

management. Kohlmeier stated, for example, that there is often political pressure on fund managers to keep the fund investments within the state or city, and to hire local bankers, brokers and investment advisers. "When this parochialism dominates investment policy," he wrote, "mortgage investment opportunities are necessarily limited, and the efficiency of security management is often restricted."[6] Kohlmeier said there is "no justification" for public pension funds being invested in state or municipal securities. These securities traditionally have offered a lower rate of return than corporation stocks and bonds because of their tax-exempt status. The earnings on pension fund investments are already exempt from taxation.

David Hall, a former governor of Oklahoma, was convicted last year of offering $25,000 to John Rogers, the secretary of state and chairman of the state retirement fund's board of trustees, to persuade the board to invest $10-million in the Guaranteed Investors Corp. After the board approved the investment, Rogers publicly revealed the bribe offer. Hall was sentenced to three years in prison. Shortly thereafter, Rogers was impeached on charges of having committed election campaign violations and other offenses. He resigned his offices before the impeachment trial, making the charges moot.

In Alabama, the 1975 state legislature made any former governor who served two terms or more eligible to receive a pension equal to the salary of the incumbent governor—$28,955 a year. The new law was passed to provide help for James E. Folsom, a former governor who has been in poor health, and to provide security for Gov. George C. Wallace, who is paralyzed

---

[6] *Conflicts of Interest: State and Local Pension Fund Asset Management* (1976), p. 53.

from the waist down. Wallace, who has warned that the state "may pension itself into bankruptcy" in future years, has proposed legislation to increase contributions to the state pension funds to make them actuarially sound.

A study by Robert Tilove for the Twentieth Century Fund[7] indicates that state and local government employees across the country often retire with benefits which he considers excessive. For instance, he said, one-fourth of those who earn $10,000 a year and retire at age 65 after 30 years of service will receive combined pension and Social Security benefits equivalent to more than what their net take-home pay was while they were still employed. If the spouse's Social Security benefits are taken into account, two-thirds of all state and municipal employees will receive more than their net pay in combined retirement benefits. Tilove said that taxpayers will refuse to support this system when they realize that public employees receive more for not working than they did for actually working.

Rising Costs in the Military and Civil Service

Similar charges of overly generous benefits have been made against the federal civil service and military retirement systems. The primary target of this criticism has been a 1 per cent "kicker" clause that was added in 1969. Retirees are entitled to a matching increase whenever the cost of living rises 3 per cent and remains at that level for three months. The increase is not added to pension checks for an additional two months, however. To compensate the pensioners for the money lost during the waiting period, the increase becomes 4 per cent instead of 3 per cent. This 1 per cent bonus becomes a permanent part of the pension and its cumulative effect is considerable.

Since 1969, the Consumer Price Index which measures the cost of living has risen 50 per cent and federal pension benefits have increased 63 per cent. As a consequence, the government's military and civilian retirees received $1.6-billion more by the end of fiscal year 1975 than they would have received if pension benefits had not outpaced the index. The 1 per cent "add on" also has generated $11.2-billion in future liabilities. President Ford asked Congress on March 24 to eliminate the added benefit. "It is neither appropriate nor fiscally responsible for the federal government to continue to provide such an added benefit," he said.

The House Subcommittee on Retirement and Employment has scheduled hearings in June on a bill sponsored by Rep. David N. Henderson (D N.C.), chairman of the parent House Post Of-

---

[7] *Public Employee Pension Funds* (1976). Tilove is a senior vice president of Martin E. Segal Co., a pension actuarial and consulting company. He served as consultant on private pension plans to the White House Conference on the Aging in 1961.

Growing Military Retirement Costs

Fiscal Year	Defense Budget Outlays (in billions)	Retirement Outlays Amount (in billions)	Retirement Outlays Per Cent of Total
1972	$ 76.0	$3.9	5.1
1973	73.8	4.4	6.0
1974	78.4	5.1	6.5
1975	86.0	7.3	7.2
1976	91.2	6.2	8.0
1977 (proposed)	100.1	8.4	8.4

SOURCE: Department of Defense

fice and Civil Service Committee, to eliminate the 1 per cent benefit but compensate retirees by reducing the waiting period from five months to two months. Another bill, sponsored by Rep. Paul Findley (R Ill.), would repeal the benefit and suspend the cost-of-living escalator provision long enough to correct for the over-compensation of beneficiaries.

Soaring pension costs in the federal government are also attributed to liberal retirement formulas. Civil Service employees may draw full pension benefits at age 55 if they have 30 years of service. In addition, retired employees are allowed to work in other jobs and still continue to receive their federal retirement checks. If they work in private industry long enough, which many do, they qualify for Social Security benefits.[8] Social Security annuities are tax-free, while federal retirement annuities are tax-free only for about 18 months.

President Ford and members of Congress have expressed concern over rising payroll and pension costs in the military services. Pay and retirement benefits account for 57.4 per cent of the $100.1-billion budget outlays proposed by the Department of Defense for fiscal year 1977, beginning Oct. 1, 1976. This is up from 42 per cent in fiscal 1968 despite a decrease of more than one-third in personnel since then. Most of the growth in pay and benefits is attributed to higher pension costs and to legislation that linked military pay to federal civilian pay raises. According to the Department of Defense, the cost of military retirement was $7.3-billion in 1975 and will rise to $8.4-billion in 1977. "Military retirement...is a key issue that has to be faced," Martin Binkin wrote in a study for the Brookings Institution

---

[8] Federal government employees are prohibited from participating in Social Security while employed by the government.

"The stakes are high; the financial consequences are potentially greater than those involved in the major debates over force levels and weapons systems."[9]

The Defense Manpower Commission advised in April that the number of service years required for retirement of non-combat personnel be increased to 30, from 20. Currently, members of the military forces can retire after 20 years of service and collect annual pension benefits equal to half of their last year's active-duty pay. Military personnel who retire by age 40 are likely to receive benefits for a period longer than they served in the armed forces. Citing indications that the military retirement system "motivates early retirement," the commission, in its final report to the President and Congress, noted that few serve beyond age 55.[10]

Development of Private Pensions

T HOUGH the voices of alarm being heard today about pensions are directed mostly at government, the problems in private industry cannot be overlooked because of its size. The Social Security Administration estimates that pension plans in private industry cover 29.8-million Americans and, in 1974, paid $12.9-billion in benefits. In contrast, public-employee plans cover 20 million persons.

Since 1974 a number of private plans have had to put more money into their reserve funds to offset future deficits. Business has tended to attribute much of its added pension costs to the 1974 pension reform act. According to Edwin F. Boynton, an actuary in Washington, D.C., the new law raised the average company's pension costs 5 to 7 per cent.

After a century of development, pension systems in private business today are closely regulated by the federal government—perhaps more closely regulated than public-employee plans. While the beginning of pensions in America can be traced to a plan established by the American Express Co. in 1875, the idea caught on very slowly until well into the 20th century.[11]

There were probably fewer than 10 private pension plans in operation in the United States by the turn of the century. Then

---

[9] *The Military Pay Muddle* (1975), p. 57. See also "Volunteer Army," *E.R.R.*, 1975 Vol. I, pp. 443-462.

[10] *Defense Manpower: The Keystone of National Security*, April 1976, p. 346.

[11] See Merton C. Bernstein, *The Future of Private Pensions* (1964).

in the early 1900s labor unions began to show an interest in providing a retirement income for their elderly members.

Originally, union plans were completely financed by the members. Organized labor approved of this arrangement since it viewed plans financed by the employer as a threat to the union. In 1927, however, the American Federation of Labor reversed its position and began to push for pension plans supported by contributions from the employer. Today, most private plans are totally financed by the employer. Union activism in the Thirties pushed industry to provide retirement benefits but it was World War II that caused the greatest spread of pension plans. Many companies decided to grant their employees pensions in lieu of salary increases since raises were being controlled by the government. Wartime profits were used to fund the plans.

"...[T]he financial consequences of military pay are potentially greater than...force levels and weapons systems."

Martin Binkin, Brookings Institution,
The Military Pay Muddle (1975)

Raymond Schmitt, a social legislation analyst at the Library of Congress, reports that from 1925 through 1949 retirement plans evolved from relatively simple arrangements into the more complicated plans of today. Three events of that period shaped the future development and role of retirement plans, he has written. "These events were the granting of tax exemption to private pension plans, the passage of the Social Security Act, and the refusal of the U.S. Supreme Court to review an earlier decision that required employers to bargain with labor unions on the issue of pensions...."[12]

The number of employee pension and welfare plans grew enormously during the postwar years. By 1949, there were over 12,000 private pensions in existence covering about nine million workers in private industry—up from four million in 1940. Until 1950, almost all private pension funds had been placed in standard, fixed-interest investments. That year, however, General

---

[12] Raymond Schmitt, "The Historical Development of the Private Pension System," Library of Congress, March 24, 1972, p. 8-9. The Supreme Court case involved a ruling by the National Labor Relations Board in 1947 that pension plans were a proper subject of collective bargaining under the Taft-Hartley Act. The Seventh Circuit Court of Appeals upheld the decision in 1948; when the Supreme Court refused to review the case the following year, the appeals court ruling was left standing.

Motors, under the chairmanship of Charles E. Wilson, began to operate its pension plan as an "investment trust" and became one of the first companies to invest pension funds in the stock market. Other plans followed GM's lead as pension coverage continued to expand during the 1950s.[13] Private pension coverage was fairly stable in size during the 1960s while benefits were liberalized.

Efforts to Curb Abuses in Fund Management

Along with the growth of pension funds came complaints of their misuse and mismanagement. Congress passed the Employee Retirement Income Security Act of 1974 in response to such complaints. They included grievances over eligibility requirements, inadequate funding by the employer, cancellation of plans that left eligible employees with no pensions, and the misuse of pension funds by the union or employer in charge. Congressional investigations during the 1950s revealed instances of financial mismanagement and plundering of funds.

In an attempt to correct these abuses, Congress in 1958 passed the Welfare and Pension Plans Disclosure Act, which required the managers of pension and welfare funds to report on their operations annually. Convinced that disclosure of plan operations alone was insufficient to ensure proper management of funds, Congress in 1962 authorized the Labor Department to investigate the truthfulness of reports, and made it a federal crime to steal from employee welfare and pension funds. However, the new law did not provide for the vesting of pension rights and did not protect eligible recipients in the event a fund went bankrupt.

Pension plans again came under public scrutiny two years later when Studebaker went out of business, leaving thousands of automotive workers jobless at its South Bend, Ind., plant. Only employees aged 60 and older with 10 years of service received full pension benefits. Younger but fully vested workers received only 15 per cent of the retirement benefits they had earned under the Studebaker plan. Many other employees received nothing.

A committee that had been appointed by President Kennedy in 1962 to study pension funds recommended in January 1965 that federal regulations be instituted to require fuller funding of private pension plans and minimum vesting standards.[14] A com-

---

[13] For background on the GM plan, see Peter F. Drucker, "Pension Fund 'Socialism,'" *The Public Interest,* winter 1976.

[14] The committee was known officially as the President's Committee on Corporate Pension Funds and Other Private Retirement and Welfare Programs. Secretary of Labor W. Willard Wirtz headed the committee, which included the Secretaries of Treasury and of Health, Education, and Welfare, the chairmen of the Federal Reserve Board, Council of Economic Advisers, and Securities and Exchange Commission, and the director of the Budget Bureau (now the Office of Management and Budget).

Chronology of Pension Fund Development

1859. New York City policemen obtain a pension fund, the first created for state or local government workers.

1875. American Express Co. sponsors first pension plan in U.S. private industry.

1893. Nation's first pension fund for public-school teachers is established in Chicago.

1905. Granite Cutters union sponsors a pension fund, the first by organized labor that is destined to last.

1920. Federal Civil Service Retirement and Disability Fund is created.

1935. Congress approves legislation to set up Social Security and Railroad Retirement systems.

1962. Self-Employed Individuals Retirement Act (Keogh Act) opens pension planning to the self-employed.

1974. Employee Retirement Income Security Act is signed into law Sept. 2.

prehensive pension reform bill was introduced in the Senate in 1967 but lay dormant. From 1969 through 1972, however, extensive hearings were held in both the Senate and House. As witnesses voiced their grievances, public interest in pension reform picked up and constituent mail increased in Congress. A bill was reported to the Senate in 1972, but the measure died in a jurisdictional dispute between two Senate committees. Then in 1974 the Employee Retirement Income Security Act was passed. It represented Congress's response to the complaints that had arisen over the past decade.

Provisions of the 1974 Pension Reform Act

The major provisions cover vesting, funding, fiduciary standards, insurance against plan terminations, tax changes and new reporting and disclosure provisions. In general, the act requires employers to contribute to their pension plans at an orderly rate so that adequate funds will be on hand to meet pension obligations. Plans in existence before 1974 must amortize their unfunded liabilities in no more than 40 years. Those created after 1974 have 30 years.

Pension plan fiduciaries are required to manage the assets of the fund "solely in the interests of the plan's participants and benficiaries." They must invest the fund assets in such a way "as to minimize the risk of large losses, unless under the circumstances it is clearly prudent not to do so." No more than 10 per cent of the assets are allowed to be in securities or real property of the employer.

173

An important provision of the 1974 act set up a Pension Benefit Guarantee Corporation in the Department of Labor to insure employees their full benefits in the event their pension plans are terminated. Pension plans must pay a premium for the termination insurance.[15] The agency can attach up to 30 per cent of a company's net worth to cover pension fund losses, and it also acts as a counselor to persons who wish to set up individual retirement accounts.

Individual retirement accounts, known as IRA's, are another feature of the act. The act allows persons who are not covered by a company pension plan to set aside 15 per cent of their annual salary or $1,500, whichever is less, for retirement savings. This money can be invested in an account with a bank, savings and loan or credit union, or in an annuity contract issued by an insurance company. It is exempt from federal income taxes until it is drawn out during retirement. At that time the taxpayer presumably is in a lower tax bracket.

In recent months, insurance companies that offer IRA plans to eligible individuals have been questioned about their selling practices. During hearings conducted by the House Ways and Means Oversight Subcommittee in November 1975, witnesses accused insurance companies of not giving customers an accurate picture of the true cost and value of their IRA plans. Critics have charged that the insurance companies' advertising in many cases has failed to mention large service charges and commission fees. On April 1, 1976, the Federal Trade Commission issued a consumer's guide to buying an Individual Retirement Account or an annuity. The FTC is investigating whether IRA advertising has been misleading.

New Requirements of Law for Vesting Rights

Provisions having to do with vesting form a key section of the 1974 act. "The largest number of complaints against private pensions came from individuals who had worked for as much as 30 years for a company but still had not qualified for a pension," Peter Henle and Raymond Schmitt wrote in their legislative history of the act. "The law attempts to remedy such conditions by setting forth specific standards for vesting, the non-forfeitable right to a pension. Once the individual becomes vested he is entitled to a pension at a retirement age based on his service, even though at that time he may no longer be working under the plan."[16] Before passage of the law, most private pension plans did provide a certain degree of vesting, but age and service requirements varied considerably. In 1974, about 20 per

---

[15] Initially $1 per participant for single-employer plans and 50 cents per participant for multi-employer plans. The rate is subject to change.

[16] "Pension Reform: The Long, Hard Road to Enactment," *Monthly Labor Review,* November 1974, p. 5.

Pension Terms

Minimum funding standards require pension managers to put aside enough money to ensure payment of workers' pensions.

Vesting guarantees a worker the right to at least some pension benefits regardless of whether he or she continues to work for the sponsoring company until retirement.

Plan termination insurance protects workers' benefits if companies go bankrupt or have underfunded their pension plans.

Portability allows employees to transfer pension benefit credits from one employer to another.

Fiduciary or *trustee standards* establish regulations for proper management of pension funds.

cent of private plans provided full vesting rights after 10 years of service.

Under the 1974 law, employers may choose one of three vesting formulas:

1. Gradual vesting in which a worker becomes entitled to 25 per cent of his or her accrued pension rights after five years of service.

2. Full vesting after 10 years of service.

3. The "Rule 45" whereby an employee whose age and number of service years total 45 is 50 per cent vested after five years of service.

All three choices require that an employee be at least 50 per cent vested after 10 years of service and 100 per cent vested after 15 years of service. The new law also mandates that all employees with at least one year of service be eligible at age 25 to participate in company pension plans. The promoters of pension regulation were disappointed that the act did not include a strong portability provision to permit workers to carry full pension rights as they moved from one job to another. "While this legislation does remove some of the restrictions hampering full freedom of employment, it does not entirely free an employee from the need to stay at one place of employment for a certain length of time...in order to have his credits vested," Rep. Michael J. Harrington (D Mass.) complained at the time of the act's passage.[17]

The law does not require employers to offer pension plans. Nor does it deal with the adequacy of pension benefits. Its thrust is to require those employers who offer plans to meet specified

[17] For a summary and legislative history of the Employee Retirement Income Security Act of 1974, see *Congressional Quarterly Almanac 1974*, pp. 244-253. See also "Retirement Security," *E.R.R.*, 1974 Vol. III, pp. 967-984.

minimum standards. The act "by no means begins to solve our retirement income problem," said Karen Ferguson, executive director of the Ralph Nader-sponsored Pension Action Project. "Pension coverage is still only provided for one-half the private work force. The only realistic supplement called for is the IRA." Noting that the law was designed to correct the "outrageous horror stories" of the past, Ferguson added that a lot of expectations will not be fulfilled.

Prospects for Retirement Security

PRIVATE industry complains of paperwork and administrative costs generated by the 1974 law[18] and of government slowness in drawing up guidelines and regulations. "We're having a number of firms with pension plans come to us and ask to serve as trustees," Randy Mott, president of First Tennessee Investment Management Inc., has said. "These executives no longer want the responsibility and liability connected with pension fund trustees."[19] Under the terms of the new law, fiduciaries can be sued for mishandling pension money.

Critics of the law charged last year that administrative costs caused by complicated reporting and disclosure regulations of the act were responsible for the termination of several thousand private plans during 1975. A recent study conducted by the Pension Benefit Guarantee Corporation indicated that the law was a factor in 23 per cent of the 4,300 terminations that year. Other factors, such as the economy, also played a role. The study noted that in 35 per cent of the terminated plans, the employer intended to set up another plan.

The report said that 3,200 plans would have ended even if the pension law had not existed. "Perhaps as many as 1,000 plans have terminated" because of the law, according to Matthew Lind, director of program and policy development for the Pension Benefit Guarantee Corporation. "But what we might be seeing is an acceleration of terminations that would have occurred anyway. Whether there's been a net increase in terminations is hard to say."[20] In the meantime, government regulators have taken steps to decrease the amount of required paperwork. The

---

[18] One of the forms originally required was 31 pages long and asked employers to write essays in response to some of the questions. The form was withdrawn by the Department of Labor immediately after it was issued in April 1975.

[19] Quoted by Bruce Sandey and Emmett Maum in the Memphis *Commercial Appeal*, March 21, 1976.

[20] Quoted by Lee Dembart in *The New York Times*, March 21, 1976.

House Education and Labor Committee has approved a bill to ease some of the fiduciary requirements of the law. Plans with fewer than 100 participants already have been exempted from annual auditing and allowed to file shorter forms.

Proposals to Regulate Public-Employee Plans

While the Department of Labor and the Internal Revenue Service work to simplify the reporting and disclosure requirements, Congress is debating whether federal pension regulation should be extended to public-employee plans. Dan McGill of the University of Pennsylvania urged as far back as 1972 that this be done. "There is a general consensus among knowledgeable persons that retirement systems for public employees are much more in need of regulation than the plans of private employers," he testified before the Senate Labor Subcommittee during hearings on the proposed regulation of private plans that year. "As a group, public employee retirement systems are inadequately funded, poorly designed, and subject to unsound political manipulation."[21] State and local officials lobbied heavily against regulation and urged Congress to hold off until further studies had been made.

"...[R]etirement systems for public employees are much more in need of regulation than the plans of private employers."

Dan McGill, University of Pennsylvania,
Senate Labor Subcommittee hearings, 1972

The Pension Task Force of the House Education and Labor Subcommittee on Labor Standards issued an interim report March 31, 1976, that criticized the management of state and local pension plans. "The absence of any external independent review [of public-employee plans] has perpetuated a level of employer control and attendant potential for abuse unknown in the private sector," the report continued.[22] It accused public pension administrators of using poor accounting methods, investing funds for purposes other than to benefit the employees, and failing to fulfill reporting and fiduciary responsibilities.

---

[21] "Retirement Income Security for Employees Act, 1972, Hearings," June 20-21, 1972, Part I, p. 208.

[22] "Interim Report of the Activities of the Pension Task Force of the Subcommittee on Labor Standards," March 31, 1976, p. v. The task force's final report is due Dec. 31, 1976.

The interim report was also highly critical of New York City for using public pension funds to help offset the city deficit. "As a matter of general policy we are convinced that such transfers from retirement programs to finance local governmental operations unduly impair the stability of the plans, substantially increase the cost of providing retirement benefits to the sponsoring employers, and reflect an absence of budgetary discipline on the part of these employers," the study said. The task force noted it had discovered "numerous instances" of governments using pension plan assets to finance municipal operations.

One result of the interim report has been the introduction of a bill by Rep. John Dent (D Pa.) and Rep. John Erlenborn (R Ill.) to regulate public-employee pension plans.[23] The Dent-Erlenborn measure, known as the "Public Service Employees Retirement Income Security Act of 1976," would establish reporting, disclosure and fiduciary relationship standards for all state and local employee pension systems but not plans sponsored by the federal government. The Dent-Erlenborn bill contains no provisions for vesting, portability or funding. A spokesman for Dent has indicated that such provisions could be added.[24]

Withdrawal of Local Units From Social Security

As Congress considers the possibility of imposing federal regulations on state and municipal pension plans, a number of the plans have withdrawn from participation in the Social Security system or have given the required notice of intent to withdraw. Citing high costs of financing Social Security, state employees in Alaska last December filed notice they wanted to withdraw. New York City followed suit on April 1. Nine million state and local workers belong to the Social Security system voluntarily and, unlike persons in private industry, may opt out. Fewer than 100,000 had done so over the years through 1975, but at the year's end 322 withdrawal notices were pending that affected more than 50,000 participants. During 1974 and 1975 most of the withdrawal notices came from California, Texas and Louisiana.

"Distrust of the Social Security system and rising costs are the main reasons why those who can are opting out," *Barron's* magazine reported in March.[25] The federal program is paying out more money in benefits than it is taking in,[26] and critics foresee a time when the cost of the system will become too great

---

[23] Dent is chairman of the House Subcommittee on Labor Standards and Erlenborn is the ranking Republican member.

[24] See "Public Pension Plans: Federal Standards?" *Congressional Quarterly Weekly Report*, May 8, 1976, pp. 1133-1135.

[25] Shirley Scheibla, "Anti-Social Security," *Barron's*, March 8, 1976.

[26] See "Social Security Financing," *E.R.R.*, 1972 Vol. II, pp. 705-724.

a burden for the taxpaying worker. America's biggest pension system of all, Social Security, appears to be the most troubled about the future.

The Social Security Administration pays $5.7-billion a month to almost 32 million retired or disabled Americans, their dependents and survivors. They represent one American in every seven, and their number is growing faster than the proportionate growth in population. Payroll-tax increases have been imposed repeatedly in recent years to finance Social Security benefits but more funds are needed. President Ford proposed in his 1976 State of the Union message that beginning next Jan. 1 the combined tax on employees and employers be raised to 12.3 per cent, up from 11.7 per cent. An election-year Congress has been reluctant to act.

When Social Security was created in 1935, state and local employees were prohibited from joining the system. In 1951, however, employees not covered by a public plan were given the option of becoming members. Four years later this choice was extended to all public employees. Under current provisions of the Social Security law, public employee groups can withdraw from the system after participating in it for seven years and giving notice two years in advance.

In giving such notice on behalf of New York City, Mayor Abraham Beame said the city could no longer support two pension systems. City workers with 10 years of service still retain their right to Social Security retirement benefits without paying further taxes to the fund. State and city officials, therefore, usually propose that the fund managers cancel coverage and use the discontinued payments to provide additional benefits. Pointing out that employees with less than 10 years of service and those hired in the future will have no rights to Social Security benefits, Tilove argues for mandatory participation in Social

---

Assets of American Pension Funds

(As of December 1975; in billions)

Private Industry		Public Employees	
Insured	$ 69.4	State and local	$106.5
Non-insured	145.2	U.S. government	
		Social Security	44.4
Total	$214.6	Civil Service	38.6
		Railroad Retirement	3.0
		Total	$192.5

SOURCE: Securities and Exchange Commission

Security for all public employees. Furthermore, he proposes that public plans be integrated with Social Security rates to prevent combined retirement benefits from exceeding an employee's salary.

Criticisms of the Federal Retirement Program

Many critics of Social Security would be opposed to mandatory participation for public employees. One observer, for example, has expressed surprise that governmental units have taken "so long to catch on to what Congress and the federal government have long known—that Social Security is no longer a 'good buy' for the average, relatively well-paid worker, and that anyone who can legally do so, will do well to opt for his own private system of retirement benefits." Writing in *The Washington Post*,[27] Jodie T. Allen, senior vice president of an economic research firm called Mathematica Policy Research, said the federal program is "no longer competitive with many private retirement systems" because it contains elements of "income redistribution." This referred to the fact that the Social Security benefit formula is weighted in favor of lower income workers.

"...[The Employee Retirement Income Security Act] should be called the Full Employment Act for Lawyers and Actuaries."

Merton C. Bernstein, letter to
The New York Times, March 16, 1976

Ronald A. Anderson, a Philadelphia lawyer and author, has formed a non-profit organization called the Social Security Citizens Foundation and is lobbying for a "People's Option Program" that would allow Social Security contributions to be made on a voluntary basis.[28] Anderson has argued that all workers should be given the choice of paying taxes into a government trust fund or a tax-exempt retirement account like the IRA or Keogh plans *(see chronology)* that have been enacted by Congress. "Just going along with the old system and raising tax-

---

[27] April 6, 1976.

[28] Social Security is now mandatory for all employees in private industry except self-employed persons and railroad workers. The latter have their own government-sponsored retirement fund.

Mandatory Retirement

A little more than one-half of all employed Americans work in jobs that force them to retire at a specified age. According to past surveys, two-fifths of those who are within one year of forced retirement would rather continue working.

Do mandatory retirement rules discriminate against the rights of older workers? Rep. Paul Findley (R Ill.) thinks so and has introduced a bill to outlaw them. The bill is pending before the House Education and Labor Subcommittee on Equal Opportunities, which held hearings on it Feb. 9.

Mandatory retirement is defended as a means of keeping the work force young and able. It is argued that employing the elderly tightens the job market for younger workers. But demographic trends may alter the nation's views. *Business Week* has warned* that by 1985 there will be fewer persons in their late forties and early fifties to fill positions in management. "Growing labor and management personnel shortages," the magazine stated, "will probably spur most companies to abandon mandatory retirement rules and, instead, find ways to keep competent older workers on the job."

The typical retirement age for workers in private industry is 65. For federal, state and local employees, it is about 70. However, for policemen, firemen and others in jobs considered hazardous, the usual age limit ranges from 55 to 65.

Col. Robert Murgia, who was forced to leave the Massachusetts State Police in 1972, has challenged the Massachusetts law that requires the retirement of state policemen at age 50. The U.S. Supreme Court is expected to rule on the case before its term expires in June.

* March 8, 1976.

es year after year is not the answer. "Social Security is not safe. It discriminates. It is not sufficient."[29]

There is little indication that Congress is willing to make Social Security voluntary for all. Major changes in the system may occur in the years ahead to meet criticism of inequities and underfunding. For the time being, however, Congress will probably be occupied with consideration of federal regulation for state and municipal pension plans, particularly as the unfunded liability of many public plans continues to rise.

---

[29] Quoted by Don Lambro in a United Press International dispatch printed in the Buffalo *Courier-Express*, May 2, 1976.

Selected Bibliography

Books

Bernstein, Merton C., *The Future of Private Pensions*, Macmillan, 1964.

Nader, Ralph and Kate Blackwell, *You and Your Pension*, Grossman Publishers, 1973.

Tilove, Robert, *Public Employee Pension Funds*, Columbia University Press, 1976.

Articles

"Belated Rules for the IRA Boom," *Business Week*, Dec. 8, 1975.

Drucker, Peter F., "Pension Fund 'Socialism,'" *The Public Interest*, winter 1976.

Henle, Peter and Raymond Schmitt, "Pension Reform: The Long, Hard Road to Enactment," *Monthly Labor Review*, November 1974.

Niland, Powell, "Reforming Private Pension Plan Administration," *Business Horizons*, February 1976.

Perham, John C., "The Mess in Public Pensions," *Dun's Review*, March 1976.

"Public Pension Plans: Federal Standards?" *Congressional Quarterly Weekly Report*, May 5, 1976.

"Why Bigger Pensions Will be Harder to Come By," *U.S. News & World Report*, March 15, 1976.

Studies and Reports

Binkin, Martin, "The Military Pay Muddle," Brookings Institution, 1975.

Defense Manpower Commission, *Defense Manpower: The Keystone of National Security*, April 1976.

Editorial Research Reports, "Public Employee Militancy," 1975 Vol. I, p. 685; "Retirement Security," 1974 Vol. I, p. 965; "Social Security Financing," 1972 Vol. II, p. 705.

Henle, Peter and Raymond Schmitt, "Private Pension Plan Reform: A Summary of the Employee Retirement Income Security Act of 1974," Congressional Research Service, Library of Congress, Sept. 19, 1974.

Institute of Life Insurance, "Pension Facts 1975," 1975.

Kohlmeier, Louis M., "Conflicts of Interest: State and Local Pension Fund Asset Management," Twentieth Century Fund, 1976.

Pension Benefit Guaranty Corporation, "Analysis of Single Employer Defined Benefit Plan Terminations, 1975," March 19, 1976.

Pension Task Force of the Subcommittee on Labor Standards, "Interim Report of Activities," March 31, 1976.

Schmitt, Raymond, "The Historical Development of the Private Pension System," Congressional Research Service, Library of Congress, March 24, 1972.

INDEX

A

Affirmative Action
Administrative expense and red tape - 151
Backlash in academia - 151
Case for preferential treatment - 148
Case for 65-year retirement age - 69
Extension of rules to education - 146, 155
Federal contract compliance - 116, 154
Job quotas controversy - 154
Preferential treatment to women and minorities - 145, 150
Reverse discrimination charges - 145
Seniority issue - 158
Supreme Court rulings - 146, 156, 158, 159
Veterans Preference Act of 1944 - 150

AFL-CIO
Entry of women workers - 112, 113
Illegal immigration problem - 127, 137
Job protection and free trade - 3
Job quotas controversy - 155
Mandatory retirement for age - 65
Minimum wage youth differential - 97
Pension plans development - 171
Retroactive seniority ruling - 160
Reverse discrimination case - 156

Age discrimination. See Civil Rights; Mandatory Retirement

Aliens. See also Illegal Immigration
Amnesty for illegal aliens - 137, 140
Braceros and green card commuters - 134, 136
Contract-worker programs - 135, 140
Deportable aliens in U.S. - 135
Legal immigration from Latin America - 139
Projected U.S. population growth (1960-2050) - 128
Push-pull factor in immigration - 130
'Texas Proviso' - 136

B

Blacks. See Minorities

Brookings Institution
Minimum wage and teenage unemployment - 95
Military retirement costs - 169
Welfare reform - 59
World's economic recovery - 23, 35

C

Canada. See also Industrial Countries
'Downing Street Summit' - 24
Green card commuters - 136

Illegal immigration problems - 130
Real GNP growth (table) - 25
Youth unemployment - 87

Carter Administration
Conflict between free trade and jobs - 3, 5, 19
Economic recovery targets - 24, 26
Humphrey-Hawkins bill - 56, 97
International economic affairs - 33
Pressure to restrict imports - 4, 5
Steel industry reference price system - 15
Welfare reform - 43, 44, 56
Wheat acreage cuts - 36
Youth employment programs - 83, 85, 87

Chase Econometrics Associates - 26

Civil Rights. See also Employment Discrimination
Affirmative action cases - 145
Age discrimination and employment - 63-65, 77
Development of affirmative action - 153
Immigration policy reassessment - 137
Sex discrimination guidelines - 116, 155

Civilian Conservation Corps - 91

Common Market. See European Economic Community

Conference on International Economic Cooperation (CIEC)
Attempts to ease poor nations' debt - 37

D

Developing Countries
"Brain drain" - 128, 138
Current OPEC countries - 30
Effect of surplus petroleum funds - 32
IMF attempts to ease oil debts - 36
Outmigration problems - 131, 138, 141
Trade protectionism increase - 6, 34
Steel industry development - 14

Discrimination. See Civil Rights

E

Economic Nationalism
Congressional 'isolationism' - 5
Effects of '74 recession - 6, 7, 23, 30
Effects of U.S. tariff policies - 8
Growth of commodity cartels - 34, 35
Movement to liberalize trade relations - 10, 34
Oil crisis of 1973 and global interdependence - 33, 38
Protectionist trade measures - 5, 6, 8, 34, 35

183

Growth of global trade - 27
Pacts for controlling commodity fluctuations - 35
Report on mid-1977 conditions - 23
Global structure of current account balances - 38
Trade protectionism pressures - 6, 23, 34
International Trade Commission (ITC)
Shoe import tariffs - 7
Television import tariffs - 18
Trade Expansion Act of 1974 provisions - 6
International Trade Organization (ITO) - 10
Italy - 25, 28, 87

J

Japan. See also Industrial Countries
Illegal aliens - 132
Japanese-American trade problems - 18
Real GNP growth - 25
Role in world economic recovery - 24, 33
Steel industry exports - 13
Tokyo Round negotiations - 11, 34
Youth unemployment - 87
Job Corps. See Federal Work Programs
Job equality. See Civil Rights
Job Protection
Alternatives to seniority-based layoffs - 161
Conflict between free trade and jobs - 3
Pressure to restrict imports - 4
Problems facing steel industry - 12
Seniority rights controversy - 158
Shoe industry petitions - 7
Job quotas. See Affirmative Action

L

Latin America
Approaches to immigration problems - 131
Illegal immigrants in U.S. - 125, 126
Immigration policy reassessments - 137-141
Push-pull factor in immigration - 130
Sources of legal immigration - 139

M

Mandatory Retirement. See also Retirement
Business, university opposition to change - 68
Congressional action to raise age limit - 63, 181
'Gray power' lobby - 66, 71
Legal-right questions before the courts - 77, 181
Organized labor's neutrality - 65

Origins of 65-year retirement age - 69
Pension problems. See Pensions
Population and income factors - 69
Trauma of retirement - 67, 68, 73
Mathematical Policy Research
Criticism of Social Security system - 180
McCarran-Walter Act of 1952 - 132
Mexico
Bracero Program - 135
Deportable aliens in the U.S. - 135
Green card commuters - 136
Illegal immigration - 125
Immigration law changes - 126
Legal immigration from Latin America - 139
Origin and characteristics of illegal aliens - 129
Push-pull factor in immigration - 130, 141
Steel industry development - 14
Middle East. See Developing Countries
Military ·etirement costs - 169
Minimum Wage
Effect on teenage employment - 95, 96
Impact of illegal aliens in U.S. - 127
Subminimum wage for youth - 97
Subsidized public service jobs - 44
Minorities. See also Aliens; Women
Affirmative action programs - 153
Blacks
Controversy over Job Corps in 1960s - 94-95
Debate over remedies for past bias - 145
Disdain for work ethic among teenagers - 89
Minimum wage debate - 96, 97
Preferential admissions to professional schools - 152
Racial hiring quotas - 154
Seniority rights - 158
Teenage joblessness - 83-90
Unemployment rates - 24, 83, 85
Criticisms of EEOC - 119
Illegal Aliens
Estimated illegal population (map) - 129
Green card system - 136
Origin and characteristics - 129
Racism and immigration policy - 138
Temporary labor contracts - 135

N

National Council on Employment Policy
Immigration policy confusion - 132
National Youth Administration - 91